EAT MY FLESH, DRINK MY BLOOD

The greatest Inheritance of power and revelation that Jesus left us

Ana Méndez Ferrell

International

DEDICATION

I dedicate this book to my beloved Father in Heaven, Jesus, my eternal bridegroom and the sweet and precious Holy Spirit and also to all my fellow workers of Voice of The Light Ministries.

EAT MY FLESH, DRINK MY BLOOD
The greatest Inheritance of power and revelation that Jesus left us

1st English Edition – 5th Printing
Copyright © 2006 Ana Méndez Ferrell

Translation:
 Jorge Jenkins
Si Señor Traducciones

Cover design:
Ruben Mariaca Asport
areyou_ben@hotmail.com

Interior design:
Stefan J. Hülf
stefanjhuelf@gmx.net

All scripture quotations unless otherwise indicated are taken from the King James Version

Printing:
United Graphics, Inc

Publisher:
Voice Of The Light Ministries
PO Box 3418
Ponte Vedra, Florida 32004 USA
www.voiceofthelight.com
ISBN 978-1-933163-11-6 (13 digit)
ISBN 1-933163-11-9 (10 digit)

CONTENT

Foreword

"Eat My Flesh, Drink My Blood" was divinely birthed in Ana Méndez Ferrell by the Spirit of the Lord. As you read this book and ponder every word, a fresh impartation will make you into a new creation which is a part of His Plan for your life.

When I began to read what Ana wrote about communion, I found myself absorbed with every word. It became obvious to me that she was not just speaking words, but that it was a living reality that had become a lifestyle for her. It not only consumed her, but had permeated the depths of her being.

Ana has an amazing revelation from the spirit of the Lord that will help us understand how everything we need in our spirit, soul, and body, is found in communion. Our precious Lord Jesus made the greatest sacrifice so that we can know and walk in the absolute healing.

When communion becomes a lifestyle, you realize that you not only want the Lord Jesus to have your heart, but also you want to be consumed by Him.

In this way His Holiness, fear and reverence of who He is can come forth to a lost and dying world. That is why Jesus came down to earth so we can know heaven on earth.

Ana has been given much insight into the fullness of this revelation and has been given a commission from the Lord to help others reach their full potential in Him. She reveals how the church not only walked in this place but also how, throughout history, men, churches and religions have allowed this precious act of adoration and worship to become a formless and meaningless ritual.

Ana tells us how it is only the Holy Spirit who teaches us all things. He is the One who puts the foundation deep within us so we can grasp the depth of the Lord and the Cross which is imparted to us by faith. When this becomes a living "rhema" revelation, not just "logos" without power or substance, that is when the spirit of the living God will join us in an intimate union as we, His Church become His bride and He becomes our bridegroom.

In our daily time of intercession, praise, worship and adoration, it is very important that we take the bread, representing His broken body and the wine or grape juice representing our total deliverance from our sins and freedom from our iniquities, that we find the time when we are totally abandoned in Him.

When we have had time to minister to Him and know that he has cleansed us afresh, then we can know that the body of our Lord becomes one within us. Whether you do it by yourself in the "secret place" or with a group of believers, it is important that communion becomes a daily living expression of your love for Him as well as His love for you.

Ana's book "Eat My Flesh, Drink My Blood" is the reason she walks in the fullness of the revelation of her Master. I have had the privilege on several occasions to participate with Ana in partaking of these Holy elements.

May the Lord open up your understanding as you read through the pages of this book.

Suzanne Hinn

Introduction

This book deals with the most important revelation of my life. What He gave me through His Spirit completely changed me. The understanding of the Kingdom of God that I received was something I had never before imagined.

This revelation has changed the lives of thousands of people. It has taken them to experiences with Christ that they never dreamt could be real. Even less could they imagine that they could have these experiences themselves, through entering the spiritual dimensions of "Communion".

This is not a religious study. It is a glorious revelation of the life that is hidden behind the bread and the wine, in the body and the blood of Jesus. I'm not trying to attack anyone, nor attempting to dispute traditions or established theology. My intention is to help you understand a mystery that will transform your entire spiritual life.

During some years of taking "Communion" the way I believe the early church took it and living the way they lived, I discovered the legacy of Christ. It is my desire to impart to you what He has given to me and for the Holy Spirit to take you to the fullness of your Christian life.

Throughout history, God has always found someone to whom He could reveal this heritage. Saints throughout the ages, in every denomination, in diverse circumstances, have found this pearl of great price. He found them in the midst of the Dark Ages. He took them out of the most perverted religious structures in the history of the church. They were isolated in a monastery or a convent or were hidden as hermits in the mountains. Others received this revelation while they were missionaries in Africa or China. These men and women were lovers of truth; they were saints who sought Him and did not seek the doctrines of men.

They separated the precious from the vile. They endured horrible persecution and even death because what they had was real. What they had was life and not some dead theology. These men and women set aside rituals and traditions; they had found Jesus face to face.

Some of them shook the earth, as well as the religious and political systems of their time. Others transformed nation from their prayer rooms because they knew the mysteries of life that are hidden in Communion.

This book will help you to know Jesus intimately. It will help you to do the works of God, with the same power the Son of God had when He was on earth. Jesus promised:

Verily, verily, I say unto you, He that believeth on me, the works that I do shall he do also; and greater works than these shall he do; because I go unto my Father.

John 14:12

It will open your eyes to see Jesus face to face, and it will help you to possess your spiritual and material inheritance. What you are about to read will change your life, your Christian experience, the way you see things, and how you love. It will fill you with the very power of God.

Open your heart to receive a treasure you have never received before. And may the Almighty God reveal Himself to you in every page of this book!

PART  *1*

The Establishment
of Communion

Our Marvelous Heritage, Lost in History

Jesus came to earth to give us the greatest inheritance one could imagine: His very life within us. Just as the Father sent Him, He wanted us to be sent, doing even greater signs and wonders than He had done while on earth. He wanted the supernatural reality and power of His kingdom to be manifested in us.

For this, He trained His disciples to appropriate for themselves all that he had conquered for us. His Apostles understood it. They not only lived it, but they taught it in such a way that the whole first century church moved in this might.

God's impact on earth was visible in unprecedented ways. His love and His power filled every Christian. Jesus was visible in each believer, and therefore, the book of Acts was being written in the midst of awesome manifestations of the Spirit of God.

Today we read about that glorious church and yearn for what they had. However, those days seem so distant. We still wonder where are the keys that opened the doors to so much power and love, and the keys to our real inheritance.

The key is hidden in the great legacy Jesus left us: the mystery of Communion. Unlike our practice today, the breaking of bread was much more than merely a ritual for the early Christians. We need to realize that everything we need is contained in that one act of Communion. That is, if we are able to properly understand it.

And they continued steadfastly in the Apostles' doctrine and fellowship, and in breaking of bread, and in prayers. And fear came upon every soul: and many wonders and signs were done by the Apostles.
Acts 2:42-43

The Apostles obviously taught them to persevere in these truths, and due to this, the fear of God and His holiness prevailed in the Church, producing so many signs and wonders.

God is speaking again today what He had revealed to those early believers, because the unity among the brethren, holiness and wonders need to be restored.

The Spirit of Religion Destroyed the Life

The early church had the pure essence of life. The Holy Spirit came upon them so powerfully that everything that Jesus was came alive in the believers. They lived a spiritual reality and a dependence upon the Holy Spirit rarely seen today. But this was lost little by little. The subtle spontaneity characterizing the life hidden in this mystery became something mechanical, contaminated by religion. What was once alive gradually became a ritual.

With the death of the founding fathers of the Church, many revelations were forgotten. Traditions and the ways of men began to spring up in the Church like weeds and thistles.

The Sacrament throughout History

With the death of the Church patriarchs, the Church lost its spirituality. It lost its dependence upon the Holy Sprit as the fountain of all divine knowledge, and it began to depend upon men. Because of the scarcity of apostolic writings and ancient testaments, obviously due to the nonexistence of the printing press, religious men of the times turned the Church into a ritualistic system. In the 4th century, it was further contaminated by the Roman Empire when Emperor Constantine fused Roman paganism and Christianity.

In the 9th century, controversy began over Communion. Unfortunately, this occurred during a time of great darkness when magic and superstition were prevalent. These influences filtered into the Church. Radertus introduced mysticism and the supernatural of his time to the Church, bringing to Rome the theory of transubstantiation. He taught that when the words of the Eucharist were spoken, the elements literally changed into the body and blood of Christ. Ratramnus, who held the Augustinian position that the Lord's presence was merely spiritual, radically opposed Radertus. Against great opposition, transubstantiation became official in the Fourth Council of 1215, and Saint Augustine's theology lost the battle.

The theories of Radertus originated in Egyptian rituals, such as those performed to the god Osiris in the Temple of Amon-Ra thousands of years before Christ. In this ceremony, the priest would invoke the spirit of Osiris with the sound of a bell, raising his arms toward a flaming star with five points. When the clear liquid in the cup of consecration changed to pink, they would know that their god had manifested himself.

This was one of the topics of greatest controversy in the period of the reformation of the 16th century. In the Council of Trent (1545 – 1563), it was added that the bread and the wine must be worshipped, as they were equivalent to God Himself. This belief is still held today in the Roman Catholic Church.

Different opinions emerged in an effort to discover the truth about this key Christian doctrine, creating conflict among the reformers. Although there were differing positions, all of them opposed transubstantiation. Martin Luther, leader of the German Reformation, wrote in *"The Babylonian Captivity of the Church"*:

"It is an error that opposes Scripture, goes against reason, is contrary to our senses of sight, smell, taste and touch. It destroys the true meaning of this sacrament and leads to great superstition and idolatry."

He also criticized the Church for denying the people access to the Communion chalice and for teaching that Communion is a sacrifice offered to God. Here the priest offers to God the very body and blood of Christ, repeating the atoning sacrifice of our Lord, but without the shedding of blood.

The true sacrament of the altar, Luther states, is God's promise of the forgiveness of sins. This promise is provided for with the death of His Son. Since it is a promise, access to God is not obtained by works or by our efforts to please Him, but by faith.

In 1524, Luther began his attack on the doctrine of transubstantiation and the sacrifice of the altar, founding his argument on Scriptures:

But Christ being come an high priest of good things to come, by a greater and more perfect tabernacle, not made with hands, that is to say, not of this building; Neither by the blood of goats and calves, but by his own blood he entered in once unto the holy place, having obtained eternal redemption for us.
Hebrews 9:11-12

Though he remained in firm opposition to these doctrines, he always agreed with Saint Augustine that during Communion the believer truly receives the body and blood of Christ.

Among the contemporaries of Luther was Ulrich Zwingli, who led part of the Swiss Reformation. He came from a humanistic background, which caused him to differ in his theology from the German reformer. Zwingli removed the presence of God from Communion, stating that it was simply a symbolic act during which Christ was totally absent.

Calvin's position fell between those of Luther and Zwingli. He maintained that there was a genuine receiving of the body and blood of Jesus during Communion, but that it occurred at the spiritual level. Like Luther, Calvin believed that the elements of Communion were signs of Christ's presence, opposing Zwingli who believed Christ to be absent. Luther and Calvin maintained that Christ was present, nourishing the believers with His body and His blood.

The Calvinist position is the one largely held by the Evangelical church, as well as the one with the greatest acceptance among contemporary Catholic and Lutheran theologians. This position states:

Holy Communion is a ritual instituted by Jesus in which bread is broken and the fruit of the vine is drunk in an act of thanksgiving for the atoning sacrifice of Christ. In this sacramental act, the Holy Spirit blesses Communion with the body and blood of Jesus, in anticipation of our future salvation.

Due to these declarations, what we have today is a ritual. We have a religious act that has virtually no effect on believers. It's a formality that is performed periodically in our churches. It's a "must do" sacrament that has completely lost the essence of what it meant to the early church.

God is calling us to go back to the beginning, to seek Him in order to find what it was that He left us by way of inheritance.

And he shall send Jesus Christ, which before was preached unto you: Whom the heaven must receive until the times of restitution of all things, which God hath spoken by the mouth of all his holy prophets since the world began.
Acts 3:20-21

Today's Church is beautiful and has powerful anointing, but falls short in the most important areas. It lacks brotherly love, the supernatural power and life of God manifested in every believer, and the fear of God that leads to true holiness. Without these three things we are just tinkling cymbals, clouds without water blown to and fro. We are the lovely façade of an empty building.

The sound emanating from the Church today is ambiguous. We preach that we have a personal relationship with Christ, but the vast majority of Christians has only a mental concept of Him, without really knowing Him. We preach about His great love and power, while the Church is fragmented and divided throughout the world, filled with gossip and destruction. It is full of sick, indebted people, and for the most part is in financial need. We preach that we love Him, the majority of believers does not seem to find keeping His commandments important. However, Jesus did say, *"He that loveth me keepeth my commandments."*

Why? One question begs to be answered: If we are supposed to have everything, why don't we really have it?

The early church walked in a profound love for one another. In Jerusalem, they became of one heart and one soul, so much so that they held everything in common. They had so much power that it amazed everyone. It was irrefutable that the supernatural presence of God manifested among them. The fear of God sustained their holy lives. For this reason the heavens were manifested in their midst. They saw angels. They were supernaturally transported from one place to another and witnessed extraordinary miracles.

The sound they produced was real. They lived what they spoke and it shook the entire world.

The reason they reached this level is that they understood the Holy Communion in a living, powerful way.

For them it was not just a ritual, but an intimate union of the Spirit of Christ with the Spirit of Man.

Through numerous years of taking Communion as they took it and through a life similar to the way they lived, I found the most important element of the legacy of Christ. In these pages it is my desire to give you what He has given to me so that you may reach the fulfillment of your Christian life.

Eat My Flesh, Drink My Blood

One day, Jesus spoke what could be the most important words concerning His legacy upon the earth. These words shook His followers and provoked absolute wrath among the religious leaders of His time. His statement made hell tremble. It would mark the difference between those who had been given to Him truly by the Father, and those who followed Him out of mere curiosity or self-interest.

"I am the living bread that came down out of heaven; if anyone eats of this bread, he will live forever; and the bread also which I will give for the life of the world is My flesh."
Then the Jews began to argue with one another, saying, "How can this man give us His flesh to eat?" So Jesus said to them, "Truly, truly, I say to you, unless you eat the flesh of the son of Man and drink His blood, you have no life in

yourselves. He who eats My flesh and drinks My blood has eternal life, and I will raise him up on the last day."

John 6:51-54

What Jesus is talking about here is a matter of life and death. It is of such importance that He risks the loss of all His disciples and ignites the wrath of the Pharisees. Jesus is giving us the key to possess our entire inheritance, and for this reason, Satan has fervently tried to rob it from us throughout the ages.

What is Eternal Life?

Jesus is the Son of God manifested in the flesh. In Him the unfathomable mystery is fulfilled, as the Creator of the whole universe becomes one with human nature. In Jesus, heaven and earth are united in the same body.

He made known to us the mystery of His will, according to His kind intention which He purposed in Him with a view to an administration suitable to the fullness of the times, that is, the summing up of all things in Christ, things in the heavens and things on the earth.

Ephesians 1:9-10

The coming of Christ marks the fullness of the times and the uniting of all things, those in heaven and those on earth.

When Jesus was conceived, the Father's nature was fused with that of the woman. Blood can only be transmitted through the seed of the man to the egg of the woman. In this case, the Father puts His life in the form of blood into the womb of Mary.

The Father used the instrument of His blood to unite human and divine nature. It is through this blood given by the Father that the blood of Jesus was formed. Eternity penetrated time and inhabited a body for the first time at Jesus' conception. This is ETERNAL LIFE. This term does not only mean life that does not die, but it has to do with the very nature of God, penetrating our humanity and uniting us with Him. The Son of God became flesh and dwelt among us, and He continues to become flesh through His body, the Church. This great miracle began during the Annunciation:

The angel answered and said to her, "The Holy Spirit will come upon you, and the power of the Most High will overshadow you and for that reason the holy Child shall be called the Son of God."
Luke 1:35

The two natures of Jesus united. The Holy Spirit operated as the vehicle, whereas the Father contributed His blood and the flesh came from the egg of Mary. The eternal life that is God Himself first became blood and then flesh.

This illustrates what Jesus was trying to say to His disciples. It is not only necessary to have faith in Me, which brings My Spirit and presence to you, but you must eat My body and drink My blood so you can received eternal life and become one with My Spirit. Just as the body needs food, your spirit also must be fed so that I can resurrect it (paraphrased).

Jesus is trying to tell us that the spirit of man needs to eat in order to live. He compares it with the supernatural walk of God's people in the desert:

Jesus then said to them, "Truly, truly, I say to you, it is not Moses who has given you the bread out of heaven, but it is My Father who gives you the true bread out of heaven. For the bread of God is that which comes down out of heaven, and gives life to the world."
John 6:32-33

Please note that in order for the Father to give life, He must present Jesus as a form of food, which is bread. All life created by God must not only be born, but must be fed. Otherwise, it becomes weak and dies. What is true in the natural is true in the spiritual.

Jesus did not speak haphazardly. His words were carefully chosen because they carried within them the Spirit of the Father. He said:

For My flesh is true food, and My blood is true drink.
John 6:55

Jesus is about to introduce an extremely powerful concept, and He chooses the every day terminology of eating and drinking. He is not talking about a ritual or a memorial. He isn't using religious words of any kind, but talks about something as simple as our daily sustenance.

Our spirit, in order for it to live and stay strong, must eat every day, just like our body. He is establishing a principle that will become a way of life, something that must be done daily. Jesus wanted to make Himself present in our spirit every day. If He were attempting to establish a ritual to be performed once a month or once a year, He would have selected different words. Eating and drinking are not annual or monthly events, but something that is ESSENTIAL and must be done DAILY.

The early Church had no problem understanding this.

Day by day continuing with one mind in the temple, and breaking bread from house to house, they were taking their meals together with gladness and sincerity of heart.

Acts 2:46

Jesus had instilled in His Apostles the importance of participating in His flesh and in His blood to keep eternal life in them. It not only kept the presence of God continually in their spirits, but it would be the basic requirement TO DO THE WORKS OF GOD.

Do not work for the food which perishes, but for the food which endures to eternal life, which the Son of Man will give to you, for on Him the Father, God, has set His seal." Therefore they said to Him, "What shall we do, so that we may work the works of God?" Jesus answered and said to them, "This is the work of God, that you believe in Him whom He has sent."

John 6:27-29

Note that the context in which Jesus talks about believing in Him and coming to Him is concerning the difficult words He was about to speak: Eat My flesh and drink My blood.

"I am the bread of life; he who comes to Me will not hunger, and he who believes in Me will never thirst."
John 6:35

His flesh is true food and His blood is true drink. He who eats and drinks of Him will do the works of God, just like Jesus. The Father who dwelt in Him is the One who did the miracles.

"As the living Father sent Me, and I live because of the Father, so he who eats Me, he also will live because of Me."
John 6:57

Jesus made it very clear that it was the Father who operated through Him, in order to do the works of God. Later in this same Gospel, we read:

"Do you not believe that I am in the Father, and the Father is in Me? The words that I say to you I do not speak on My own initiative, but the Father abiding in Me does His works."
John 14:10

Like the Father's supernatural life operated in Him, Jesus wanted His supernatural life to operate in us; this is His inheritance for us. For this, our spirits need to abide in Him, by eating and drinking everything He is. Through this abode, our prayers would always be heard and the miraculous power of God will flow through us.

> *"He who eats My flesh and drinks My blood*
> *abides in Me, and I in him."*
> *John 6:56*

Just as eating and drinking are things that we do every day, so is abiding, which means a permanent dwelling place where we live every day.

Jesus, speaking later on in His teachings about this abode, said:

"I am the vine, you are the branches; he who abides in Me and I in him, he bears much fruit, for apart from Me you can do nothing. If anyone does not abide in Me, he is thrown away as a branch and dries up; and they gather them, and cast them into the fire and they are burned. If you abide in

Me, and My words abide in you, ask whatever you wish,
and it will be done for you."
John 15:5-7

How are we to abide in Him? We abide in Him by eating His flesh, drinking His blood and keeping His commandments. The power of prayer increases in a great way as we remain in His presence. This is the place where all prayers are answered, where all things are done by the Father. When the church understands this awesome principle, it will conquer the world.

How Does This Great Mystery Occur?

Man was created to live, move and have dominion in two dimensions: one dimension is material and the other is spiritual.

We are essentially spirit. We live in a body, and we have a soul, which is the instrument through which we communicate in the natural world. The spiritual world is fed from that which is spiritual, and the natural world from that which is earthly.

When we enter the kingdom of God through genuine repentance and commitment to follow Jesus Christ as Lord and Savior, the Spirit of God unites with the spirit of man, transforming him into a new creation. From that moment on, he will grow and be strengthened through spiritual food, which is the flesh and blood of Jesus, as well as the Word of God.

When the elements are sanctified for Communion, Christ is powerfully present among us. This is not a ritual or a memorial. It's something real that occurs in the invisible world.

The elements of the bread and the fruit of the vine will always remain bread and the fruit of the vine, but in the invisible realm, the body and blood of Jesus are really there. Our spirit will literally drink of His blood and will become one with His flesh and His body. Our spirit will absorb the very life of God and everything that is contained in that flesh and that blood. God and man will blend little by little together until we are totally consumed within Him, and He within us, becoming one spirit.

> *But the one who joins himself to the Lord*
> *is one spirit with Him.*
> *1 Corinthians 6:17*

This is what the early church believed. That is why the works of God were so amazing during those days. Communion was not a religious sacrament. It represented the very life of Jesus. This life was so visible within them, and the works of God were seen everywhere. They were like the light of a fisherman when he casts it out in the waters in the middle of the night, attracting multitudes of fish.

They could not bear the thought of losing that wonderful grace, that hope of Glory, Christ living and working through them. The fear of God kept them in holiness and in profound love for one another, and this brought about the first great harvest of souls.

They were continually devoting themselves to the apostles' teaching and to fellowship, to the breaking of bread and to prayer. Everyone kept feeling a sense of awe; and many wonders and signs were taking place through the apostles. And all those who had believed were together and had all things in common; and they began selling their property and possessions and were sharing them with all, as anyone might have need. Day by day continuing from house to house, they were taking their meals together with gladness and sincerity of heart, praising God and HAVING FAVOR WITH ALL THE PEOPLE. AND THE LORD WAS ADDING TO THEIR NUMBER DAY BY DAY THOSE WHO WERE BEING SAVED.
Acts 2:42-47 (Emphasis by the Author)

Spiritual Food and Drink

So Jesus said to them, "Truly, truly, I say to you, unless you eat the flesh of the Son of Man and drink His blood, you have no life in yourselves."
John 6:53

When the Lord speaks to us about eating or drinking something spiritual, it has to do with appropriating it for ourselves. It means making it a part of our life and of being, saturating our spirit, soul and body.

In the Word we have various examples in which God provides spiritual food and drink to some of His servants, and even to His own Son. Their experiences enable us to see the effect this food and drink had on their lives.

One of these men is the prophet Elijah, who is strengthened by food impregnated from heaven, as he escapes from Queen Jezebel in order to save his life.

He lay down and slept under a juniper tree; and behold, there was at his head a bread cake baked on hot stones, and a jar of water. So he ate and drank and lay down again. The angel of the Lord came again a second time and touched him and said, "Arise, eat, because the journey is too great for

you." So he arose and ate and drank, and went in the strength of that food forty days and forty nights to Horeb, the mountain of God.
1 Kings 19:5-8

The angel of the Lord is none other than Jesus prior to His coming in the flesh. He shows up and gives Elijah a meal. This meal affects his being to such a degree that it literally drives him in a supernatural journey to the mountain of God.

Something extremely powerful happens to Elijah's body upon eating that food. The cake is natural bread, like the Communion bread, but since it is given to him by the angel of the Lord, the spirit of Elijah is filled with the supernatural power of God. Elijah not only performs the physical exploit of walking for 40 days without rest all the way to Horeb, but that meal leads him to a unique encounter with the Father.

Notice that the decision to go to the holy mountain of God does not proceed from the mind or fearful heart of Elijah, but is inspired by the angel, who sustains him by means of that bread from heaven.

There are divine encounters awaiting us, revelations reserved by the Father that will only come through the divine food that only Jesus can give us.

When Elijah embarks upon his journey, he does not know his destination, but that bread held the path of his steps, leading him to a face to face encounter with God. There, his ministerial legacy and the invisible work of the Most High will be revealed to him via the 7,000 chosen ones who will carry out the Lord's plans.

Eating His flesh is much more than feeding oneself. It is entering into dimensions with God that transforms our very being and our understanding.

My husband and I take Communion almost every day. Many times angels descend in order to give us that supernatural food.

God has led me to climb many mountains in spiritual warfare to free entire regions from the power of the enemy. Each morning before beginning the ascent we take Communion. Strength from on high comes and nurtures our whole body, and we experience a supernatural vitality that overcomes any fatigue.

One time, in an intercession mission in Iraq, the Lord sustained us day and night for 15 days without sleep. We carried out long walks under a heat of 105°F (40½ °C) and the only power that upheld us was His.

My husband fasts like no one I have ever known. There have been years in which he has fasted more than 200 days. On extended fasts that lasted 40 or 50 days, angels have descended to feed him with a meal of light, after receiving Communion. These experiences and so many more are part of our daily lives because we have discovered the spiritual reality contained in the elements which give life, power, and vital energy to our physical body.

In their pilgrimage through the desert prior to entering the Promised Land, God's people were supernaturally sustained. The Father provided for them bread from heaven and water that flowed without ceasing from a rock. This was a symbol of the spiritual food that Jesus would give us in His flesh and His blood. This nutrition in the spirit is the only thing that can sustain us and carry us to our Promised Land, which is a supernatural life, where heaven is a tangible reality. The Israelites did not get sick. Their clothing and their shoes did not wear out, even growing on the bodies of the children and teens.

The bread and the water caused the supernatural kingdom of God to descend among them. This is what happens when we consume this true food and this true drink.

For I do not want you to be unaware, brethren, that our fathers were all under the cloud and all passed through the sea; and all were baptized into Moses in the cloud and in the sea; and all ate the same spiritual food; and all drank the same spiritual drink, for they were drinking from a spiritual rock which followed them; and the rock was Christ.
1 Corinthians 10:1-4

Eating and drinking this food is going to have an effect in the spiritual world, as well as in the natural. These two verbs have to do with appropriating something that comes from God and making it 'flesh within us'.

When the Apostle John is given a little book to eat, in his visitation to heaven as described in the book of Revelation, God is implying that John should appropriate the truth contained in those revelations. He should make them his own to the point that they become part of his very being.

Then the voice which I heard from heaven, I heard again speaking with me, and saying, "Go, take the book which is

open in the hand of the angel who stands on the sea and on
the land." ... I took the little book out of the angel's hand
and ate it, and in my mouth it was sweet as honey; and
when I had eaten it, my stomach was made bitter. And they
said to me, "You must prophesy again concerning many
peoples and nations and tongues and kings."
Revelation 10:8; 10-11

This little book was a meal containing the revealed Word for the end times. All Word that proceeds from the mouth of God is food. That is why Jesus said:

And Jesus answered him, saying,
"It is written, That man shall not live by bread alone,
but by every word of God."
Luke 4:4

The word that John was receiving was sweet because it came from heaven, but it made his stomach bitter because it contained the judgment and wrath of God. John had to make the pain and indignation of the Father his own so he could prophesy with authority and truth.

Another spiritual drink we find is when Jesus had to drink God's cup of justice containing His wrath against the sin of humanity.

So Jesus said to Peter, "Put the sword into the sheath; the cup which the Father has given Me, shall I not drink it?"
John 18:11

Drinking from this cup would affect His entire being. In His soul and body it would carry sin, ungodliness, iniquity and every abomination of mankind. In His spirit, it would carry the immeasurable pain with which mankind had pierced the Father's heart.

In a wonderful description of this moment, Gene Edwards writes in *The Day I Was Crucified:*

"The cup spit its vile poison until its entire contents impregnated the winds of the earth. I observed as all the sins of the sons of Abraham ran through it. I looked at the centuries of rebellion, idolatry, incest, murder, lies and deceit. All the sins of the Hebrew race became one with it."

In this cup Jesus would bring from heaven to earth the sacrifice He had prepared before the foundation of the world. What had happened in heaven would now manifest in the sufferings of Christ. When one drinks from heaven, the plans of God impregnate the earth. In this case, the design of the Father was Jesus' own death on the cross.

What I am trying to point out with all of this is that spiritual drink and spiritual food affect one's entire being. It is not a dead symbol, but rather a link that unites heaven and earth.

In heaven there are different types of food and drink, and each type gives us a part of God, opening to us wonderful revelations and encounters with Jesus Christ.

The Bible talks about the water of life that satisfies the thirst of both the spirit and the soul.

The Spirit and the bride say, "Come." And let the one who hears say, "Come." And let the one who is thirsty come; let the one who wishes take the water of life without cost.
Revelation 22:17

This water of life, as we will see later, is connected to the Spirit of God and to the blood of Christ. It will have its effect in us when we understand the way in which these three operate. When the blood is revealed to us, with its power, its outreach and everything it contains, we will be led to the fountain of life in order to drink from it.

For there are three that testify: the Spirit and the water and the blood; and the three are in agreement.
1 John 5:7-8

In the kingdom of God there are also exquisite drinks, such as drinking the new wine of the Spirit. Jesus tells His disciples about this wine that must be put into new wine skins, referring to the time in which they would drink of the Holy Spirit (Ephesians 5:18).

As you come to understand the wonderful mysteries hidden in Communion, doors of knowledge will begin to open. Some of those doors have to do with the New Jerusalem that will descend from heaven, but that is also already within us. Jesus said that the kingdom of God is within us because where God dwells that is where His kingdom is. Within it is found the Tree of Life, which is Jesus, from which we learn to eat in order to live in perfect health.

On either side of the river was the tree of life, bearing twelve kinds of fruit, yielding its fruit every month; and the leaves of the tree were for the healing of the nations.
Revelation 22:2

The Bible also talks about abominable drinks pertaining to the kingdom of darkness, which tries to emulate the kingdom of God and its principles. One of these drinks is the chalice of fornication of the great harlot of Revelation.

The woman was clothed in purple and scarlet, and adorned with gold and precious stones and pearls, having in her hand a gold cup full of abominations and of the unclean things of her immorality... For all the nations have drunk of the wine of the passion of her immorality, and the kings of the earth have committed acts of immorality with her, and the merchants of the earth have become rich by the wealth of her sensuality.
Revelation 17:4; 18:3

During Paul's time the Gentiles participated in a ritual in which they drank from a cup and ate bread, sacrificing it to wooden idols.

What do I mean then? That a thing sacrificed to idols is anything, or that an idol is anything? No, but I say that the things which the Gentiles sacrifice, they sacrifice to demons and not to God; and I do not want you to become sharers in demons. You cannot drink the cup of the Lord and the cup of demons; you cannot partake of the table of the Lord and the table of demons.

1 Corinthians 10:19-21

So drinking and eating are symbols of something real in the spirit. These are acts that link the spiritual world with the natural world. Through these acts, the Spirit of God or demons, whichever is the case, exercise profound influence in people's lives.

PART  2

The Mystery of the Blood
in Communion

Blood in the Spiritual World

Why is blood so important to God? And what does it mean in the spiritual world?

Blood is the first element of atonement that God reveals to man. From the time of the fall of man to the revelation of the glorious future of the Church, we see God's continual intervention, a scarlet thread woven throughout Scripture, and this thread is the blood. We will never reach fulfillment, spiritual peace or total victory, without understanding the powerful mystery of this element.

The high priest of Israel must enter the Holy of Holies of the temple once a year to make atonement for the people in order to reconcile man with God. Concerning this event the Word says:

"But into the second, only the high priest enters once a year,
not without taking blood, which he offers for himself and
for the sins of the people committed in ignorance."
Hebrews 9:7

From the time man fell into sin in the Garden of Eden, he has found himself separated from God. Sin puts an end to the plan of God, distancing Him from His beloved creation. That is why God hates sin so much, because it blocks our communion with Him. God had to provide something so powerful that it would redeem everything that sin had destroyed. It must also satisfy His wrath and cry of His own righteousness that demands payment for transgression. Only one thing held this power: the love of God flowing from the very fountain of redemption through the shedding of Jesus' blood.

This blood was typified through animal sacrifices offered to God in the Old Testament as a foreshadow of Christ, the perfect sacrifice. The victim took the place of the sinner. One life was taken instead of another.

Abel was the first priest and prophet to whom God revealed the power of the blood. Abel's life was devoted to offering sacrifices to Jehovah. At that time, man did not eat meat yet; this began at the time of the flood. Therefore, the only reason Abel cared for a flock of sheep was in order to offer the sacrifice owed to God. From those days on the only way to approach God was through blood. It is still the same way today.

Without this precious element, man cannot receive from God. He cannot receive His blessings, His communion, His revelation, or His power. This is the first law for man to come to God. Without this sacrifice, Enoch would never have been able to be caught up to heaven, and Noah would never have been able to hear God. Noah knew what he had to do. After the flood, he sanctified the earth, offering a sacrifice to God.

Then Noah built an altar to the Lord, and took of every clean animal and of every clean bird and offered burnt offerings on the altar.
Genesis 8:20

The new earth was then consecrated, and the first commandment of God was given:

Only you shall not eat flesh with its life, that is, its blood. Surely I will require your lifeblood ...
Genesis 9:4-5a

Blood is something that belongs to God and therefore cannot be taken lightly. There is something profound in it that God looks at. There is something that God designed within blood that has His seal, and for that reason, must be respected.

One life is taken to save another life! This is the principle behind every atoning sacrifice. It's also the principle through which Christ redeemed us.

This principle is seen in the first Passover. In Egypt, God told Moses that the angel of death would pass over, killing every first born. Jehovah then commanded them to sacrifice a lamb and to put its blood on the lintels of the doors.

For I will go through the land of Egypt on that night, and will strike down all the firstborn in the land of Egypt, both man and beast; and against all the gods of Egypt I will execute judgments – I am the Lord. The blood shall be a sign for you on the houses where you live; and when I see the blood I will pass over you, and no plague will befall you to destroy you when I strike the land of Egypt.
Exodus 12:12-13

Here, God establishes an everlasting foundation: Those who are under the protection of the blood of the sacrifice cannot be touched by death. It was not enough to kill a Passover lamb and shed its blood. The blood must be applied to the lintels of the doors. Likewise, it is not enough that Jesus shed His blood. The blood must be applied to the lintels of the door of a man's heart, which is his spiritual house. This is done through drinking His blood.

Jesus said:

Behold, I stand at the door and knock; if anyone hears My voice and opens the door, I will come in to him and will dine with him, and he with Me.
Revelation 3:20

This door is our innermost being, and this meal is the new covenant in His blood.

It is through blood that God executed judgment upon Egypt which is a symbol of the world and the life of sin therein; He literally pulled His people out from under the yoke of Pharaoh. This is what Communion does through the blood of Christ. It brings judgment upon sin, destroying it in our lives and leading us into a new walk with Him.

It is in this walk that the tabernacle of His presence is going to be built within us, as it was in the desert. Between leaving Egypt and entering the Promised Land, God must build His dwelling among men and establish His law in the hearts of His children. The blood then continues flowing on its way to the most inward parts of our being. The blood will not just be a sign of salvation on the lintels of our hearts, but it must be poured upon the altar, sanctifying all of our soul, mind and will. From there is must be taken to the Holy of Holies, which is our spirit. The blood must run through and sanctify our inner being, so we can become the dwelling place of the Most High.

It was very clear in the old covenant that this holy place could not be entered except through the blood. The strongest and purest communion with the presence of God can only be accomplished through the union of His blood with our spirit.

He who eats My flesh and drinks My blood abides in Me,
and I in him.
John 6:56

The Contents of the Blood

God's Life is found in the Blood

Blood is the element in which life is found. And it is the origin of this life that determines its value. The Bible establishes:

For the life of the flesh is in the blood, and I have given it to you on the altar to make atonement for your souls; for it is the blood by reason of the life that makes atonement.
Leviticus 17:11

When we look at the lives of animals, we find that the larger they are, the more valuable their lives are as a sacrifice. A turtledove has a certain value while an ox has a greater value. It is the same way among men. For pagans who sacrifice human beings, a maiden has a certain value while a firstborn son has a greater value. But without a doubt, the most valuable blood is that of the only begotten Son of God.

The life in the blood is described by the Greek word *zoe*. Everything that breathes and is alive possesses the *zoe* of God. This is the essential energy that characterizes every living being. Nevertheless, *zoe* is not the nature of the Most High.

Jesus was conceived of the very life of the Father, possessing everything that God is. But He also had His mother's *zoe*, and this is the life that made him a mortal being.

Who (Jesus) although He existed in the form of God, did not regard equality with God a thing to be grasped, but emptied Himself, taking the form of a bondservant, and being made in the likeness of men.
Philippians 2:6-7

The life of Jesus with perishable substance was transformed into resurrection life, when He conquered death and was raised from the dead. The life that now flows in His blood is life that cannot die.

When Jesus descended into hell, the life in His blood was full of the glorious power of the Spirit of God. The mortal, corruptible substance of His human body was transformed at its deepest biological levels. From this moment on, the blood and the Spirit of God united to bring about the greatest miracle in history: the resurrection of Christ.

Now the God of peace, who brought up from the dead
the great Shepherd of the sheep through
the blood of the eternal covenant...
Hebrews 13:20

The union of that glorious blood with the Spirit of God produced the power that pulled Jesus out of the grave, defeating death and hell. The invincible power of the resurrection penetrated the redeemed body of Jesus. The life in His blood became the most powerful inheritance that He could leave us.

Paul lived this reality in his own flesh and in the fullness of his spirit. This is what he was trying to transmit to us. He knew that drinking from the blood of the covenant was not a ritual or a tiny sip of liquid that disappeared within ten minutes. He knew that his entire being was impregnated with this vital fluid. The blood of Jesus penetrates our spirit and invades our whole body, transforming our soul and flooding every cell of our body. The strength of His might is at work in us through His resurrection. Paul prayed for our eyes to be opened to this reality and for us to truly understand the inheritance that Jesus left us.

I pray that the eyes of your heart may be enlightened, so that you will know what is the hope of His calling, what are the riches of the glory of His inheritance in the saints, and what is the surpassing greatness of His power toward us who believe. These are in accordance with the working of the strength of His might which He brought about in Christ, when He raised Him from the dead and seated Him at His right hand in the heavenly places.
Ephesians 1:18-20

We just read that, thanks to His blood, the power of the Spirit of God raised Jesus from the dead. This dynamic power now operates within us. Jesus wanted us to drink of His blood in order to give us this wonderful inheritance.

One day I had a glorious experience that transformed my whole concept of that life in Jesus' blood that is now part

of me. I had just taken Communion, and I w
meditation on my Lord, when my spirit v
Holy of Holies in Heaven. The Ark of the Cove...
It was full of a shining energy that is difficult to describe. It
was like an incredibly dense, churning fire. Rays of light
beamed out of it.

Then I saw Jesus enter in. I could only see His white,
glistening clothing. His face was hidden behind the shining
glory that surrounded Him. A formless mass, like a wafting,
floating liquid was in front of Him, moving towards the Ark.
It was His Blood.

Suddenly, He puts it upon the mercy seat, between
the two cherubims that guard the cover. A magnificent
power was produced in that instant. It was like seeing the
explosion of an atomic bomb. Everything shook fiercely in
heaven and on earth. An endless thunder filled the entire
place.

The power that came forth from the Blood in the Arc
reached me at that moment. I felt as if thousands of volts of
electricity were going through me. My entire body turned
red. His blood was in every atom of my being. The power of
the Arc was now upon me. I saw it circulate as if there were
hundreds of lightning bolts running through my body. I
thought I was literally going to die. It was much too

ⅰverful for a mortal, ordinary being like me. His voice esounded strongly, saying, "My Father has received My Blood and now, it has united with His spirit. Receive the life in My blood." Something that I did not understand was happening that would change everything I knew about His blood.

I came back from the experience and found myself again in my bedroom, but everything within me was different. I would never again think of the blood of Jesus as a ritual, or a verbal proclamation, as I had learned. It was something that would lead me to a deeper understanding and knowledge of God.

Peter's writings about the divine life began to make much more sense. It was like finding a vein of gold in a mine that I just had to follow.

Seeing that His divine power has granted to us everything pertaining to life and godliness, through the true knowledge of Him who called us by His own glory and excellence. For by these He has granted to us His precious and magnificent promises, so that by them you may become partakers of the divine nature...

2 Peter 1:3-4a

Partaking of His blood and His flesh were leading me to a deeper knowledge of God. His life was invading my spirit each day. The rivers of the water of life flowing from my inner being began to be real. The first thing they filled up was my soul and then my body. This began to positively affect my health, strength and energy levels. I had a new vitality, and many times, even the youth could not keep up with my rhythm of life.

Being in contact with His life and united with His nature were also filling me with light, which again opened a new horizon to me.

The Light of God Is Found in His Blood

All things came into being through Him, and apart from
Him nothing came into being that has come into being. In
Him was life, and the life was the Light of men.
The Light shines in the darkness, and the darkness did not
comprehend it.
John 1:3-5

The life of God is liquid light that runs through the veins of Jesus. This light is visible in the spiritual world and is greatly feared by darkness. The light in Jesus' blood is what transforms the spiritual realm and strips the devil of his strength.

Darkness, the arena in which satan and his hosts operate, lacks substance. Its best definition is the absence of light. When we turn on a light, darkness is automatically dispelled. Just as a fish needs water to live, the devil needs darkness to survive. Exposing the devil to the light of God is the same thing as taking a fish out of the water. It loses its strength until it dies, or in the case of the devil, he falls defeated.

I began to understand that by drinking the blood of Jesus, His light ran through my veins, and I became a fearful adversary for the devil. The kingdom of darkness realized that I was aware that the light within my spirit was intensifying as I took Communion. This filled the devil with terror. I would no longer be a prey for him, nor would I fall into his deceivers' traps so easily.

After taking the Lord's Supper, I frequently spend long periods of time meditating in my spirit, basking in that marvelous light that emanates from His life. At times, I am in such unison with God that I have seen the glow of my own spirit.

God allowed me to climb Mount Everest in order to consecrate it for Him and to tear down strongholds of the devil that were holding many nations captive from that location. During the expedition, we had a very unique experience with the light of His presence. We had to hike for nine days through the Himalayas in order to arrive at our headquarters at base camp. Some days the journey took us 12 hours. On one of those days, we climbed a peak that seemed to be endless, 5,000 feet without stopping. Some of the intercessors, who would remain halfway up the mountain in order to cover the expedition in prayer, were inexperienced climbers. They began to slow our progress tremendously. Night fell upon us, and we had no flashlights, since we were supposed to have arrived at our planned destination by mid afternoon. We could not see anything at all.

There were cliffs everywhere, and it began to rain. The situation was critical because there was no one whom we could ask for help. We began to pray for a miracle, which was the only thing that would save us. Suddenly, something wonderful happened. Light began to emit from our own bodies, illuminating our way. It was a dim, bluish light, but it permitted us to see where to take our next step. It was an awesome experience.

At the beginning of the 20th century, the Lord raised up John G. Lake, one of the most powerful men in the history of the kingdom of God. He was an American missionary in Africa. He was known for the extraordinary gift of healing that moved in his ministry. His holiness and knowledge of God have inspired great ministries of today.

John G. Lake practiced Communion daily, and this greatly affected his physical and spiritual life. Many missionaries went to Africa in those days and died of different diseases that were rampant on the black continent. Nevertheless, John never got sick. This attracted the attention of some investigators, who requested a sample of his blood for analysis. They wanted to discover what it was that kept the missionary in such good health. They took the sample and added all kinds of germs of the most dreadful sicknesses. His biographers say that his blood emitted light that burned up the germs. The life of God had become one with the missionary's blood.

Light has another characteristic, it enlightens our understanding. His light shines in our inner being and leads us to glorious revelations of the hidden mysteries of God. In my book *Seated in Heavenly Places*, I talk about how to become beacons of light in great detail. Life, light and the love of God are intimately tied to His blood.

The Love of God is found and manifests in The Blood of Jesus

God is Love. That love was contained in the Father's blood that entered into Mary's womb at His Son's conception. Jesus was born carrying the mark of the love that surpasses all understanding.

This love gives all without reservation. This is the Father's nature, giving of Himself and giving without measure. God's love is the door to everything that He is and to everything He possesses.

God created man due to love. He needed a being like Himself into whom He could pour His essence of love. This is how we were created; to be the most beloved thing that He had.

Love is fullness. Where love is there is peace, joy and complete satisfaction. There is no desire, achievement or goal that contains all that love provides to the spirit and soul of man. Even the body receives benefits, filling it with a health and vitality that only love brings to life.

Love is not a feeling. Man cannot create it because it is of divine origin. Love is a person. It is Jesus incarnate. He wants to live through us and fill the earth with love. He is the Teacher and the Provider of perfect love. That is why He said:

By this all men will know that you are My disciples,
if you have love for one another.
John 13:35

His blood contains this wonderful love, and as we drink it, we become more and more filled with it. We begin to understand Him and desire Him more than anything else in the world. Love lives and beats through the blood of Jesus. It helps us to love where it is difficult to do so. It leads us to hate all separation because this is what Jesus did: He loved those who had trespassed against Him, closing the breach between God and man and reconciling us again with the Father.

The Scripture says that the blood of Jesus speaks. It cries out to God for having been shed. But it is the love contained within that blood that gathers us up and brings us to Jesus. His love groans for us because He cannot tolerate being separated from the object of His love, placing His very life on the line.

And to Jesus, the Mediator (Go-between-Agent) of a new covenant, and to the sprinkled blood which speaks (of mercy,) a better and nobler and more gracious message than the blood of Abel (which cried out for vengeance).
Hebrews 12:24 (Amplified)

The maximum manifestation of the Father's love is that He gave His only begotten Son as a sacrifice for our sins. His love for us was greater than the pain He felt when He saw Jesus brutalized and put to death on the cross.

Since love requires its beloved, love does not reject; love redeems. Love has good will towards men. It focuses, not on defects, but on virtues. It doesn't consider our deeds as important, but rather who we are to Him. He suffers and exposes Himself to reproach every day, so that He can be the unchanging banner of love over us.

Love doesn't close its heart in the face of our betrayal, indifference and contempt. It appears each morning, sweet and tender, always trying to make up. It is kind. It's always looking for ways to do good, to please, to woo a pleasant moment. With tenderness it tries to file off the rough places.

Love has long-lasting endurance. It is patient and kind. It never demonstrates envy and never boils over with jealousy. It doesn't brag or show off. It doesn't have displays of haughtiness. It isn't proud or arrogant. It is not rude and is never unmannerly.

Love is not selfish. It doesn't demand its rights or its manner of doing things because love doesn't seek its own way.

Love is not irritable. It doesn't feel threatened or hold grudges. It doesn't rejoice in injustice or desire to do evil. It rejoices when truth and right prevail. It is not offended. It takes no account of a wrong.

Love endures everything. It is always ready to believe the best of every person. It is full of hope and faith at all times. It always remains strong in any situation. It is infinitely sacrificial and is a giver without limits. It is brave, a fighter, and is not intimidated in the face of any enemy. It does not give up; it wins. In it there is no fear. It can do anything, and nothing can stop it. Love shreds to pieces fierce foes, and conquers tempestuous rivers in its desire to save one who is drowning. Love is courageous. It demolishes insurmountable walls. It changes hearts of stone into hearts of flesh. It has thousands of unreachable paths, and where there is no way, it creates one.

Love never fails. It never decays, never becomes obsolete, never abandons the cause, and never ceases to exist. Love cannot be overcome by anything or anyone. Love is the most powerful force in the universe. It is the purest manifestation of His Being. It is what makes God visible and tangible on earth.

This is what we drink when we partake of His blood. This is what we are converted into, and what we appropriate for ourselves when we make that love ours every day. The blood of Jesus fuses with our own, as we allow Him to live and to express His love to a lost world.

His love is liquid fire, running through our veins. It makes us do things that we would never do under other circumstances. It's a zeal that burns for lost souls. It is like a giant magnet, pulling us toward those in need and those who want to feel that they matter to someone else. It is God's greatest force. His love compels us to make any sacrifice. In Him, we can accomplish exploits, giving no thought to the price that we must pay.

Natural man can only aspire to a cheap imitation of the true love found in Christ, which has the power to conquer all. Man's love is conditional. It's incapable of the level of sacrifice and inner death required in order to love with one's whole heart.

Within the blood of Jesus runs this incorruptible form of the Father's love. From the time Jesus was a boy, His blood continually spoke to him about sacrifice. Every time

Jesus saw the lambs being offered upon the altar of the temple, His blood spoke to him about the love sacrifice into which He would be converted. He was the Lamb slain before the foundation of the world. This was like a seal within his own bloodstream.

Drinking His blood makes us a pleasing sacrifice upon the altar. It gives us the strength and conviction of loving as He loved, of giving as He gave, of sacrificing as He sacrificed. When we feel that it is impossible to love someone, drinking His blood will change our feelings and transform our heart.

Drinking His blood leads us to forgive the unforgivable. When we take Communion, and we have not been able to reach the freedom of true forgiveness, the sacrifice of the cross comes between us and that person who has hurt us. Jesus, forgiving from the cross, will become flesh within our being. We will not only forgive, but we will want to do something beautiful for that person. That is how He loved and forgave us.

Drinking His blood leads us to see as He sees, always seeing possibilities where natural man has lost all hope.

The Power of the Blood of Jesus

Jesus' blood has power because it is intimately linked with God's glory. It is the only tangible manifestation of the perfect life of the Father. It was at the same time human and divine. It was celestial and physical. Within it, Heaven and Earth were united. In Jesus, God and man became one.

When this substance entered the Holy of Holies in heaven and settled upon the mercy seat, God's glory became one with man. The man Jesus was the first being of flesh and bone to contain the power of His glory.

For it was the Father's good pleasure for
all the fullness to dwell in Him.
Colossians 1:19

His blood continues to release power, judging and destroying everything that opposes the righteousness of the Most High. It is a burning fire that the devil cannot endure.

The blood of Jesus contains all the authority of God. It speaks of His victory. It reminds the devil how Jesus' sacrifice unleashed the power of God upon hell, taking from the devil the keys of authority over the earth and mankind.

... Do not be afraid; I am the first and the last, and the living One; and I was dead, and behold, I am alive forevermore, and I have the keys of death and of Hades.
Revelation 1:17b-18

When we drink His blood, our spirit is flooded with that glorious power. From it, our soul drinks, and then our body, until our entire being is saturated with undefeatable power.

Since my husband and I drink and eat this spiritual food, almost every day our level of revelation and spiritual experiences with God has greatly increased. The light of that blood enlightens and opens the kingdom of God before us, and we are transformed more and more into His image.

But we all, with unveiled face, beholding as in a mirror the glory of the Lord, are being transformed into the same image from glory to glory, just as from the Lord, the Spirit.
2 Corinthians 3:18

Sometimes, as we enter deeply into prayer, we can see ourselves saturated and submerged in that blood. It is as if we were soaking in a bathtub of blood and our entire beings were being filled with it. We see the current of His strength like thousands of tiny lightning bolts going forth from it, filling us with His power.

This is not simply a matter of pleading His blood. We must have a continual, invigorating fellowship with it. The issue is that the blood needs to fill our lives completely.

Many people have been taught to plead the power of the blood of Jesus, but within themselves they don't have a living experience with that blood. The Holy Spirit has taught us that it is not what we say that has power, but the spiritual position from which we say it.

The book of Acts relates the story of the sons of Sceva, who tried to cast out a demon in the name of Jesus about whom Paul preached. The name of Jesus had no power within them, because Jesus did not dwell in their hearts.

Our spiritual position is what gives substance to our words. It is different to be filled with Jesus' blood and then proclaiming its power than speaking something that is lifeless within our spirit.

The Blood Has the Power to Open that Which Is Impossible

There, submerged in His blood, the voice of God is so clear. The blood speaks in many different ways. The heavens open because the blood has the power to open everything that stands in its way. It is a torrent of power so great that at times I have seen it as a high caliber explosion, opening the way like a turbulent river of fire, leveling everything in its path and tearing down the devil's strongholds in the spiritual world. Jesus' blood opens the way so that God's plans can be established upon the earth. It is an advancing force that tears down walls and levels down mountains. The blood destroys everything that stands against the will of God.

When Jesus gave up His Spirit and the spear pierced His heart, water and blood flowed from His side. However, in the invisible world, an extremely powerful beam shone forth that ripped the veil of the temple. The closed path between God and man had finally been opened.

The blood penetrated hell and opened the doors of death. Sheol was filled with the victorious power of the blood of the Lamb. The chains that bound us began to break, falling off as they felt the power of His blood. Everything remained desolate in hell and then Jesus took the keys of death and of Hades. Everything began to tremble as if shaken by the reverberating effects of an explosion. The blood opened the way so that Jesus could ascend in resurrection. The power arrived all the way to the tomb and removed the stone. The veil of the temple was torn, and the tomb was transformed into the reflection of the Holy of Holies in heaven. God's glory filled everything, and the splendor of the resurrection shone from the tomb in all its power. Two cherubs guarded God's presence over the Ark of the Covenant, and two angels showed up to make His glory accessible to all men. The blood opened the heavens, so that they could be revealed to God's children. In this way, His children could be translated to Heaven in this life and in the one to come.

The blood is still the channel that unites us with the dimensions of Heaven. At times, God has given me the privilege of going to the third Heaven before His Throne, as well as to other celestial places pertaining to the kingdom of God, as He did with the Apostle Paul. (I say this in all humility, without comparing myself in any way to the great Apostle.) Each time this has happened, it has had something to do with being submerged in His blood.

The blood of Jesus has an opening power, like a master key that opens the mysteries of God.

That their hearts may be encouraged, having been knit together in love (in His blood that reveals His love), and attaining to all the wealth that comes from the full assurance of understanding, resulting in a true knowledge of God's mystery, that is, Christ Himself, in whom are hidden all the treasures of wisdom and knowledge.
Colossians 2:2-3 (Part added)

The Finished Work is Revealed in Each Way the Blood Was Shed

Each one of the seven parts of Christ's suffering in which His blood was poured out are doors to hidden mysteries that open and reveal themselves in fellowship with His blood. The cross is an infinite paradise of blood droplets, each one full of light and revelation. It is the entrance to the Heavenly City, to the dwelling places of the Spirit and to celestial places.

Thousands of experiences of deep knowledge and revelation are before the believer who finds this master key, and dives into this river of light.

The Blood In the Sweat of His Forehead

Victory over all pain and suffering of the soul is found in those drops in the sweat of His forehead. The power that submits our will to that of God is found there. We can drink of those same drops, and make any desire that opposes God to submit to Him. These are drops of blood that take us to unprecedented levels of intercession. They attract God's angels to help us die to ourselves and assist us in passing tests of purification that, without His blood and His angels, would be impossible to get through.

Father, if You are willing, remove this cup from Me; yet not My will, but Yours be done. ...And being in agony He was praying very fervently; and His sweat became like drops of blood, falling down upon the ground.
Luke 22:42; 44

The Blood that Flowed from the Slaps and Blows that Disfigured His Face

The blood that flowed from the slaps and blows that disfigured Jesus' face gives us triumph over pride and vanity, and rescues us from the yoke of reproach and rejection. It gives us the power to endure when people humiliate and mock us. It allows us to be like Him during the loss of our reputation. It helps us to see the celestial and divine side found when the beauty within us has been destroyed in order for His beauty to shine through our being. When the soul and the spirit are full of this beauty, men's words no longer matter.

Many times, God has asked me to love those who have destroyed me with their mocking and reproach. Drinking this blood has strengthened my heart in order to love and love and love again, where natural man no longer has that capacity.

Then they spat in His face and beat Him with their fists; and
others slapped Him, and said, "Prophesy to us,
You Christ; who is the one who hit You?"
Matthew 26:67-68

... They humiliate Israel's king, slapping him around like a rag doll.

Micah 5:1b

Just as many were astonished at you, My people, so His appearance was marred more than any man and His form more than the sons of men.

Isaiah 52:14

The Blood Shed When Pieces of His Beard Were Pulled Out

His beard speaks of the priesthood. Through this blood we reclaim the lost priesthood that permits us to minister before His presence. It is from Jesus' beard that His anointing descends upon his entire body, as it occurred with Aaron, the high priest.

It is like the precious oil upon the head, coming down upon the beard, even Aaron's beard, coming down upon the edge of his robes.

Psalm 133:2

I gave my back to those who strike Me, and my cheeks to
those who pluck out the beard; I did not cover
My face from humiliation and spitting.
Isaiah 50:6

The Blood Shed During the Whipping that Tore His Back

We drink the victory over all disease in our physical body as we drink this blood. Just as Jesus took away our sins, He suffered in order to carry in His body all our sickness and pain.

Jesus was never sick while He was on the earth. He was a man without sin, and this protected His body so the devil could not touch Him. satan can only touch fallen nature due to sin. The prince of evil wanted to destroy Jesus with all kinds of sickness, but he could not. When He was on the cross, Jesus covered Himself with sin. This attracted to Himself all sickness and He carried it to death, through His own death. This is one of the most powerful things that happened at Calvary and that gives us the possibility of living a life full of health. It would be difficult for a body continually washed with the blood of Jesus to become sick. God is calling us in this generation to enter and possess all that Jesus did for us through His sacrifice.

Surely our griefs He Himself bore, and our sorrows He carried; Yet we ourselves esteemed Him stricken, smitten of God, and afflicted. But He was pierced through for our transgressions, He was crushed for our iniquities; the chastening for our well-being fell upon Him, and by His scourging we are healed.
Isaiah 53:4-5

When my husband and I are attacked in our physical bodies, instead of running to the doctor, we cling to the power that is in the blood and in the flesh of Jesus. We look at His wounds and His shed blood and we decree, believing with all our hearts that these wounds were not in vain for us. He gave the death sentence to all sickness, and we should believe it and drink in that blood our own victory over all sickness.

The Blood Produced by the Crown of Thorns

This blood crowned Him as King of kings and Lord of lords. It gave Him the victory over the devil's empire. He conquered the government of the earth. This gives us the position of kings and the ability to govern with Christ. This blood conquered strongholds in the spiritual world and in the mind of man. By drinking this blood, we conquer our thought life so we can have the mind of Christ. We appropriate for ourselves the conscience of Christ.

Jesus the man believed everything that was written about Him. He knew that everything He was in His spirit had to invade His entire human nature until He became the Christ in His whole being. He trained His mind to be subject to His Spirit in order for Him to see Himself as He really was. He was Christ, the Son of God. Likewise, through fellowship with His blood, we allow the truth of who we are to penetrate our mind, until we literally become everything that is written about us.

...We are taking every thought captive to the obedience of Christ (through the weapons of the Spirit).
2 Corinthians 10:5b (paraphrased)

And after twisting together a crown of thorns, they put it on His head, and a reed in His right hand; and they knelt down before Him and mocked Him, saying, "Hail, King of the Jews!" They spat on Him, and took the reed and began to beat Him on the head.
Matthew 27:29-30

The Blood Shed from the Wounds Caused by the Nails

From this blood we obtain triumph over iniquity, over sin, over the twisted, crocked way of our footsteps. This blood opens the way of righteousness, restoring the paths of our destiny. It opens roads to carry the Gospel where there is no path or any way to get there.

... By His knowledge the Righteous One, My Servant, will justify the many, as He will bear their iniquities.
Isaiah 53:11b

For your hands are defiled with blood and your fingers with iniquity.
Isaiah 59:3a

It is the blood that also heals the earth contaminated with our iniquities.

On earth you weigh out the violence of your hands.
Psalm 58:2b

The Blood Shed from His Side When Pierced by the Spear

Fellowship with the blood of Jesus is going to allow us to know Him intimately. It will begin to transform us so that we are able to penetrate the most sensitive parts of His heart. This is one of the greatest privileges to which a human being can aspire. God will only open this part of His being to those He considers to be His bride. His bride is the one who desires Him above all. She goes wherever He goes. She follows Him because of who He is, and not because of what He can bless her with.

John was the only disciple who had the grace to arrive at this depth. He loved Jesus more than the others. He followed Jesus to the cross, while the others hid for fear of losing their own lives. The fear caused by the Roman army didn't matter to him. He just wanted to be close to his beloved; with his presence and with his eyes John wanted to give the message, "You are not alone; I'm with You to the end. If being here will cost my life, with pleasure I'll die at Your side."

When I take Communion, many times I meditate in each one of these ways in which His blood was shed, and I make them mine. In the cross there is so much richness. There are doors to inexpressible encounters with God.

Many people hear about the cross and about the need for them to surrender everything there. However, they experience fear and pain, as if something vital is going to be taken away from them. What they do not know is that when we let go of the little we have, of the corrupt parts of our being, of the things we love on earth, we enter the place where all things are redeemed and perfected. We penetrate chambers where we bond with the Lord, where all things are given to us and all prayer is answered. This is the greatest place we could ever be seated.

When God gives us the privilege of opening His heart to us, we understand His compassion in a way that will become part of our being. When the sharp edges of sin tear Him to bits, we will be sensitized to the deep pain He feels. We will be saturated with a mercy that can only come from God.

We will understand that in heavenly places there are different levels of seeing and experiencing God, from the clear, beautiful manifestation of Jesus' face to the unfathomable regions of His glory where Moses entered when he hid in the cleft of the rock.

Through His blood, and our desire to conform ourselves to God's heart is how He reveals the heavens and the riches of His kingdom to us.

The Blood Conquered the Devil

Prophetic Vision of the Power of the Blood of Jesus

It was during the first time I was caught up into the heavens that I understood the glorious power of the blood of Jesus. I was desperately in love with Jesus. I wanted to see Him, touch Him, love Him with my entire being. My heart was dying to be with Him in a different, deeper way than I had so far.

Once I was worshiping in the church of which I used to be the pastor in Mexico City, when a kind of cloud of the Holy Spirit surrounded me. Suddenly I was taken to another dimension and I was no longer in the earthly realm. I was surrounded by light everywhere. The light was alive, and it moved as if doing a dance in which the reflections and flashes made all sorts of light effects before my eyes.

Unexpectedly, from within the glimmering lights, a glorious figure appeared that looked like the Son of God. I was before Jesus. Without a word, He extended His hand and an enormous drop of blood the size of a melon appeared floating above my head. Then He said, "Drink!" I opened my mouth and drank it in one big gulp. Then a second and a third drop of the same size showed up, and He commanded me to drink them. Upon drinking the last one, I fell onto my back, and I noticed that my body had turned red. It was full of the blood.

The Lord remained before me, surrounded by those shining lights. Then, He made a signal with His hand, and a demonic creature appeared that immediately tried to climb on top of me. When the demon touched my body, from the blood within me, a consuming fire went forth and instantly destroyed it. I was dumbfounded.

Then, He made me get up. I was still full of that blood everywhere, inside and out. Next, He made some type of tissue appear before me that looked like a tumor. He said, "This is a mortal illness. I want to show you the power of My blood upon it. Don't be afraid. Open your mouth, and eat it. When I had done it, the tumor was burned up instantly as it came into contact with the blood. I was amazed. Then He said, "Eat My Flesh and drink My Blood because I will give you great victories against evil and against sickness."

Then I looked and saw that from His body shone a fire that did not burn Him. It was like looking at pure energy, churning within His being. He stopped in front of me. I had my hands raised. He put His hands over my hands and then His face in front of mine. His heart was pressed against mine. Then He said, "The time is coming when I will come upon My people, hands upon hands, eyes upon eyes, mouth upon mouth, heart upon heart." In that instant, a powerful energy went forth from His body, His face and His hands and saturated me. I thought that I would die. The force that penetrated me was so powerful that I thought I'd burst right there. In that moment, my spiritual heart was pierced by that power, and an intense pain invaded my heart of flesh. It was then that I returned to the earthly dimension.

Six hours had passed, but the people of the church had not left my side. They were waiting for me to return from the ecstasy in which I was found. Only God could have made them stay there because nothing like this had ever happened to anyone there before to help them understand what was happening to me. I was on the floor without being able to move; the weight of His glory was so heavily upon me.

A demon-possessed woman was there that day in the congregation and she approached me. I remember that just by touching her, the demon screamed and left her.

I could not get up, but I could talk. So I began to call the members of my church one by one in order to impart into their hearts the power that shone within mine. We will never forget that day.

What occurred in that ecstasy became a pillar of faith and trust in the blood of Jesus. From then on, talking about the blood and pleading it as a weapon against the enemy would have a much greater meaning for me.

A few years later, I had an experience that if it had not been for the concept I had of the blood I would not have gotten through it. I was returning from a trip of intercession in Poland where we prayed in the concentration camps of Auschwitz and Treblinka. We waged spiritual warfare in order to liberate that nation from the spirits of death that had remained there after the Holocaust of the Jews.

One night after my return to Mexico, I suddenly awoke with the feeling that an evil presence had entered my room. My heart beat wildly, and as I opened my eyes, I saw satan before me. His body and his wings filled most of the room. His face was red and full of protruding black veins. His teeth were ferocious, like those of a wolf about to attack. His body was black and slender. His wings were like those of a dragon and appeared to be made of fire. His eyes were yellow with intense black pupils. He looked at me with hatred and with the determination to kill me.

I stared at him and, to my own surprise, my whole being entered into absolute peace. With total tranquility I asked the Holy Spirit what I should do. He responded, "Manifest the Blood of Jesus that is within you."

At that moment, I saw my body turn red again, totally saturated with that wonderful blood that conquered the devil on the cross. I then put my total focus on the power that is within that blood. Suddenly, it began to shine. A powerful blast of power left the blood, like a lightening bolt of fire that literally electrocuted the devil, making him flee from my presence.

The room was filled with the presence of God. My body was without any strength, due to the vast quantity of virtue that had left me. At the same time, my entire being rejoiced at the marvelous victory that the Lord had given me.

Again I thought about that verse that says:

And they overcame him because of the blood of the Lamb and because of the word of their testimony, and they did not love their life even when faced with death.
Revelation 12:11

God's army of the last days will be a people who truly understand the blood, warriors full of this power in their spirits, and totally undefeatable. The devil greatly fears those who understand this mystery.

The Blood Speaks

The Word of God says that the blood speaks. The blood of Abel spoke of revenge, as we saw before, and the Blood of Jesus speaks of mercy.

Blood has a very special sound in the spiritual world. The innocent blood of martyrs cries day and night for God to bring them justice. Their blood is before the Father's throne as a memorial that will unleash judgment upon the empire of evil.

The Word says that the Son of God was manifest to destroy the works of the devil. The blood of Jesus is the greatest element of intercession with which Jesus prays for us before the Father.

When the blood of Jesus is manifested in the kingdom of darkness, it produces a sound of judgment so strong that it terrorizes the devil's armies. That sound opens the densest darkness in order for God's presence to be manifested.

I remember a powerful experience that occurred at the end of the 1990's. A guerilla movement had risen in the state of Chiapas in the southeast of Mexico. Thousands of Christians were murdered by the terrorist group. The blood of our brothers cried out throughout the country. The pain over what was happening kept me awake at night, while I spent whole nights in intercession.

The government had denied all foreign ministers access to that state due to the bloodshed. The pastors wanted to take advantage of the crisis in order to advance the work of the Gospel to the people who were suffering there. They wanted to bring in the evangelist Alberto Mottesi for a large evangelistic crusade, but they could not obtain the required permits.

The Lord spoke to me and said, "They have conquered him with the blood of the Lamb, with the word of their testimony, and not loving their lives in the face of death. (Revelation 12:11) Go and manifest the Sound of My blood in the heart of the conflict in Chiapas."

Obeying His word, we rented the bullring of San Cristobal de las Casas and called forth the people of God. That night was extraordinary. I saw how the sky became red as if a veil of His blood covered the city. What I was seeing was physical, but in the spiritual world I knew that His blood was descending in order to accomplish something wonderful. We began to worship, exalting the Blood of Jesus. When the anointing was at its peak, the Lord told me, "Now prophesy that the sound of the blood of the martyrs that is over the city will manifest." I did it and then we were silent.

A sound began to arise from the earth. It was like an echo in the bullring coming from thousands of Indians. I could see it with my spiritual eyes. It was rising up as it was trying to touch the mantel of Jesus' blood that covered us. There was great expectation. Suddenly, the sound and cloak of His blood became one in the sky. An explosion of power was felt, and God filled the place with His presence. Thousands of people fell on the ground; they were full of the anointing of God. The heavens had opened in an extraordinary way. To God be the glory!

From that day on, the terrorist movement began to dissolve. The doors were opened, and the government gave permission for Brother Mottesi's crusade. There was a great harvest due to the manifested Blood of Jesus.

Sometimes we have to do things we don't understand in our natural minds, but the kingdom of God is not of this world. The Blood of Jesus speaks about mercy to the Father, speaks judgment to the devil, and about righteousness and holiness to us. When we drink His blood, His righteousness and His holiness become part of us. We are filled with light in order to see our hidden sinful areas and our erroneous motives, and we are filled with the fear of God.

They were continually devoting themselves to the apostles'
teaching and to fellowship, to the breaking of bread and to
prayer. Everyone kept feeling a sense of awe; and many
wonders and signs were taking place through the apostles.
Acts 2:42-43

The Blood Conquered Iniquity, Rebellion and Sin

These three things are the power structure that the devil establishes within man through the seed with which he contaminated our nature after the fall.

Iniquity is the root of evil implanted in man that produces in him the desire to sin. Sin is the fruit that is produced when iniquity is active. Rebellion is the power that feeds iniquity so that it is continually inducing man to sin.

The finished work of the cross puts an end to this whole structure of demonic power.

But He was pierced through for our transgressions, He was crushed for our iniquities; the chastening for our well-being fell upon Him and by His scourging we are healed... by His knowledge the Righteous One, My Servant, will justify the many, as he will bear their iniquities.

Isaiah 53; 11b

We have to understand that the work of the cross is absolute. What Jesus did, He did once and for all, but it is our responsibility to APPROPRIATE FOR OURSELVES what Jesus conquered for us on the cross.

For example, Jesus died for all sinners. However, not all men are saved. Each person has to come to the Lord in repentance, and receive for himself Jesus' atoning sacrifice. If this does not occur, the absolution of the cross will not operate in that person.

This is true for each part of the cross. That is why the Lord provides us with a wonderful key in order for us to own everything that He did for us. This key is eating His flesh and drinking His blood. When a person comes to the light and walks in light, the blood of Jesus cleanses him from all sin (1 John 1:7).

When the Apostle Paul in his letter to the Corinthians institutes the Lord's Supper, he tells us to examine ourselves before taking the elements. He tells us to get things right with God, to come to the light in order to be cleansed by His blood.

When a believer has to struggle to separate himself from sin, it is due to a strong presence of iniquity in his life. Many times this iniquity is strengthened by unclean spirits that make the battle more difficult. The solution is to take the step of repentance, desiring with your whole heart that the power of God will free and transform you. This determination of the heart, together with the blood and flesh of Jesus, will give the believer total victory. The authority of the resurrection is established in every true believer so they can cast out every tormenting demon.

Later in this book, I will discuss the power of His flesh to conquer sin in greater detail. But for now, I want you to understand how the blood operates in this context. The blood has a cleansing, purifying power that penetrates the deepest roots of iniquity in our lives. But in order to experience such complete victory, we really need to actively apply the blood.

The same way that natural blood has a purifying power to eliminate toxic elements and waste, the blood of Jesus also cleanses us from all that is unclean.

In the natural, blood cleanses the body and provides it with nutritive substances such as oxygen. Blood purifies, feeds and regenerates our whole body. In the spiritual, the blood of Jesus pulls out every root of iniquity, destroys strongholds in our inner man and provides us with the elements of life and power that will carry us from glory to glory.

When a Christian struggles for holiness, the blood he drinks day after day through Communion, will regenerate him. Sin will not only be destroyed, but the Lord through His blood is going to feed us His will. Our sinful desires change into good, holy desires. The irresistible urge to do evil, to lie, to pursue fleshly desires is exchanged for the urge to do good and to draw nearer to God.

The Blood of Jesus Pulls Sinners from the Power of Hell

Vision of the Blood and the Fire

Years ago, the Lord began to speak to me about three final manifestations of the Holy Spirit. The prophet Joel prophesied about the outpouring of the Spirit of God, which was partially fulfilled on the day of Pentecost.

Even on My bondslaves, both men and women, I will in
those days pour forth of My Spirit and they shall prophesy.
And I will grant wonders in the sky above
and signs on the earth below, BLOOD, AND FIRE,
AND VAPOR OF SMOKE.
Acts 2:18-19

Here the Scripture is not talking about nuclear catastrophes, as some think. It is talking about the outpouring of the Holy Spirit. The blood, fire and smoke were three elements present in the tabernacle when the Lord manifested.

On the day of Pentecost, the Spirit came through fire, in the form of burning tongues above the believers' heads. But the smoke and the blood were not seen. Those are reserved for the complete fulfillment of the end times.

I was meditating on what this might be like while I was on a ship in the Mediterranean, and the Lord allowed me to see a wonderful vision. I was returning from my first visit to Jerusalem. My heart broke as I saw the abominations and idolatry taking place in the holy city. I went upstairs to the highest deck of the ship. It was night and the sky was full of stars. It was the same firmament that Abraham saw thousands of years ago, when God gave him the promise about how innumerable his generations would be.

I cried for the thousands of souls still held captive by the devil who need to know Jesus. As I was praying, the Spirit of God took my spirit and caught it away between heaven and earth.

Suddenly, I saw myself suspended in the stratosphere, and I could clearly see the earth, gigantic below my feet. I saw the continents, Europe, part of Asia and part of Africa. They were black as coal, and they breathed like a weak person fighting for his life with his last breaths.

Suddenly, I saw an enormous whirlwind of fire that appeared below the continents and thousands of souls were sucked up by it. They were pulled towards hell. Then, I could see fat women with Bibles in their hands that were swirling down to the pit. They screamed full of torment.

I asked Jesus who these fat women were. He told me, "They are entire churches, full of mental knowledge, but immersed in sin. They talk about Me, but they don't know Me. I spoke about them when I was on the earth:

Not everyone who says to Me, 'Lord, Lord,' will enter the kingdom of heaven, but he who does the will of My Father who is in heaven will enter. Many will say to Me on that

day, 'Lord, Lord, did we not prophesy in Your name, and in
Your name cast out demons, and in Your name perform
many miracles?' And then I will declare to them,
'I never knew you; depart from Me,
you who practice lawlessness.'
Matthew 7:21-23

When I saw this, my heart fainted inside of me. I wanted to do whatever was necessary to stop them from going to hell. Then a gigantic Cross appeared in the sky above the continents at the mouth of the whirlwind. It was so big that it was larger than the earth, and stood all the way up to where I was. The Cross was made of fire and blood. These two elements revolved and emanated from it.

Then a powerful force came out of the Cross trying to absorb everything towards it. Even the continents seemed to be swallowed up by the Cross. Thousands of people were attracted to it, and the strength that went out from it was much greater than that of the whirlwind of fire.

Then I saw the earth covered by the Blood of Jesus, while the Cross continued to exercise its power. I saw billions of people who inhabit the planet. All without exception had a portion of that blood upon their heads that cried for their salvation.

I saw the Holy Spirit slowly descending upon the whole earth, and there was a blast of thunder in Heaven that said, "I will pour out My Spirit upon all flesh!" In that moment, the Spirit made contact with the Blood that covered the planet. The effect of an atomic bomb was made that filled all the continents with power. Millions of people arose and were absorbed by the enormous Cross. More thunder was heard in Heaven, and out of it came a voice that said, "I am grafting into My Cross my true servants. They will manifest My Power from the Cross, and the Power of My Blood and the Fire of the Spirit will be seen in them. I am calling My sons and My servants to enter the Cross of My Power."

When the vision ended, my spirit returned to the ship. From then on, this experience has motivated my life to live and preach the power of the Cross.

Having canceled out the certificate of debt consisting of decrees against us, which was hostile to us; and He has taken it out of the way, having nailed it to the cross. When He had disarmed the rulers and authorities, He made a public display of them, having triumphed over them through Him.
Colossians 2:14-15

PART

**The Mystery of
The Body of Christ**

Jesus Came to Establish His Body
upon the Earth

God has given Jesus, the second Adam, all dominion and authority not only on earth, but also in Heaven. His mission is to establish His Father's Kingdom in every nation. And to do this, He needs His body, which is composed of us.

As we have already seen, the Spirit of God unites with us through Communion, making us one with the Father and the Son. The Lord imparts His own Life to us and grafts us into His body.

For by one Spirit we were all baptized into one body,
whether Jews or Greeks, whether slaves or free,
and we were all made to drink of one Spirit.
1 Corinthians 12:13

The Word of God says in Ephesians 4:10-14 that as Jesus ascended to Heaven, He filled all things, establishing His mystical body upon the earth.

Jesus' will is that His body will grow until it reaches all the fullness that is in Him. This will occur when all its members are operating in perfect coordination. Jesus is watching the finished work from Heaven where He is the head. We are His body, moving in harmony with Him.

Upon losing the essence of Communion, we lost the supremacy of the body. The body became divided and remained dismembered on earth. We try to unite it through thousands of sermons, which only serve to make us feel guilty, but lack the unifying power that only comes from eating His flesh.

Paul prayed for our eyes to be opened so we could see and understand who we are and what it means to BE HIS BODY.

The reality of being His body does not mean that you are members of an organization, or that you have a pass to Heaven. Being His body is a powerful truth. It means literally being Jesus on earth, with all His authority and virtue.

Do not cease giving thanks for you, while making mention of you in my prayers; that the God of our Lord Jesus Christ, the Father of glory, may give to you a spirit of wisdom and of revelation in the knowledge of Him. I pray that the eyes of your heart may be enlightened, so that you will know what is the hope of His calling, what are the riches of the glory of His inheritance in the saints, and what is the surpassing greatness of His power toward us who believe. These are in accordance with the working of the strength of His might which He brought about in Christ, when He raised Him from the dead and seated Him at His right hand in the heavenly places, far above all rule and authority and power and dominion, and every name that is named, not only in this age but also in the one to come. And He put all things in subjection under His feet, and gave Him as head over all things to the church, which is His body, the fullness of Him who fills all in all.

Ephesians 1:16-23

This is one of the most powerful passages of the New Testament. However, if our eyes are not enlightened to live in the power of this truth, we will keep acting like church-going Christians who have lots of problems, believing that God sometimes hears us and at other times does not hear us.

What is the key for the enlightenment of our eyes, so we can change our limited sight? It is the breaking of the bread of Communion that reveals Christ in His glory.

On the road to Emmaus the disciples walked with Jesus and heard Him speak. But although His anointing revived their spirits, they didn't recognize Him. This is how many Christians walk. They are next to Jesus. They can hear Him and feel His Spirit, but they do not really understand that they are truly with Him and in Him as His very body.

Upon breaking bread, Jesus reveals Himself to us and within us.

While they were talking and discussing, Jesus Himself approached and began traveling with them. But their eyes were prevented from recognizing Him... When He had reclined at the table with them, He took the bread and blessed it, and breaking it, He began giving it to them. Then their eyes were opened and they recognized Him...
Luke 24:15-16; 30-31a

Jesus had a purpose for causing this blindness and then lifting it. He wanted to establish the importance of the greatest heritage that He was leaving to us, the breaking of the bread.

Eating His flesh will open the eyes of our understanding so we will know all the riches that He has granted to us, so we can see Him face to face. Seeing Him is not the privilege of a few; it is our heritage, and it is what transforms us into His image.

After a little while the world will no longer see Me, but you will see Me; because I live, you will live also. In that day you will know that I am in My Father, and you in Me, and I in you.
John 14:19-20

Note in these two passages how our spiritual eyes are open. Then, we can see Him and look at Him. We know that we are truly one spirit with the Lord. When our eyes are opened, our whole perspective of things will change.

Discerning the Body of the Lord

That Jesus came to establish His body upon the earth is of great importance, because this is how God implants His designs in us. It is through His mystical body (us) that He governs and brings His kingdom to earth. Discerning the body correctly is essential to our relationship with the Father.

The New Testament apostles wanted to make sure that we understand what it means to discern the body of the Lord. To be ignorant of the body or to misunderstand it will result in illness, weakness or even the death of our physical bodies.

Today, this is one of the big problems we see. The body of Christ is mutilated, divided in all parts of the earth. Thousands of Christians are sick and many die because they attack or destroy the body of the Lord which is the Church.

1 Corinthians , Chapter 11 is one of the passages most frequently used during the actual ritual of Communion. However, it is also one of the most misinterpreted.

For I received from the Lord that which I also delivered to you, that the Lord Jesus in the night in which He was betrayed took bread; and when He had given thanks, He broke it and said, "This is My body, which is for you; do this in remembrance of Me." In the same way He took the cup also after supper, saying, "This cup is the new covenant in My blood; do this, as often as you drink it, in remembrance

of Me." For as often as you eat this bread and drink the cup,
you proclaim the Lord's death until He comes.

1 Corinthians 11:23-26

Taking Communion every day began to open my eyes to the wonderful truth in this passage. The first thing that the Spirit showed me is that the body of the Lord was broken for us. This not only speaks of His great love for the world, but it puts us in the arena of understanding what our sins produced in the physical body of Christ.

Once, while eating of His flesh, I saw Him nailed to the cross with His open wounds and disfigured face. I could see each one of my sins in each one of His wounds with my name written on them. Then, I heard His voice clearly say to me, "This is My body which was broken because of you."

A horrible shudder ran through my being when I realized that my sins crucified the Son of God. I, Ana, with my deeds brutalized my beloved Jesus. I put Him to death. We killed Him. The understanding of this fact brings us to genuine conversion.

This is what the Apostle Peter, full of the Holy Spirit, spoke to the Jews on the day of Pentecost:

"Therefore let all the house of Israel know for certain that God has made Him both Lord and Christ—this Jesus whom you crucified." Now when they heard this, they were pierced to the heart, and said to Peter and the rest of the apostles, "Brethren, what shall we do?"

Acts 2:36-37

When we understand that each one of us has killed Him, and when we see plainly that our own sins have pierced Him, then our souls will be filled with pain; and it is this that produces true repentance. How could I see my sinful works cruelly wounding Him and then go back to these sinful works and commit the same sins again?

The primitive church lived this every day. As they broke bread among the brethren, they remembered what their sins had done to the body of the Lord. They gazed into each others' eyes as they broke bread, and they saw how they had wounded Jesus' body. Their souls lived it every day. They felt it in their hearts, and it transformed them.

In Hebrew, the words "in memory of me" mean vividly reliving an event, as if it were happening in that moment. Breaking bread daily in their houses was something that deeply impacted their way of life, the way they thought, loved and knew Jesus. It affected their way of relating tore one another and even the way they treated unbelievers. The Fear of God abounded in their lives. The Holy Spirit was able to do all kinds of signs and wonders in an environment where everyone walked in holiness. Simple disciples like Ananias were led by the Spirit to amazing prophetic levels. This was used to take the Gospel to the great persecutor of the Church, Saul of Tarsus, who also was healed and received the Holy Spirit through him. Saul was impacted by this unknown brother, and is transformed into one of the greatest apostles: Paul.

Being a Christian during that time was something visible, tangible and to be admired. They had the favor of the people because believers were people full of God's love. People wanted what they had. Their greatest concern was not having the comforts of this world at any cost. It was that everyone would know the powerful Savior that had transformed their hearts.

The story of the Last Supper continues by saying:

For as often as you eat this bread and drink the cup, you proclaim the Lord's death until He comes.
1 Corinthians 11:26

The proclamation of the Lord's death means talking about His death and understanding it in relation to our own deeds. It means understanding and talking about what our sin did to Jesus, about how our iniquity led Him to die.

We literally need to eat this knowledge until everything we do and think is saturated with His sacrifice, so His life will manifest through us. It is His death that conquered death and the devil's empire.

Always carrying about in the body the dying of Jesus, so
that the life of Jesus also may be manifested in our body...
So death works in us, but life in you.
2 Corinthians 4:10; 12

Turning Communion into a lifeless ritual brings upon us the opposite effect. Judgment, sickness and death come upon the church. That is why we see so much sickness among believers, both physical and spiritual.

Therefore whoever eats the bread or drinks the cup of the
Lord in an unworthy manner, shall be guilty of the body and
the blood of the Lord. But a man must examine himself, and
in so doing he is to eat of the bread and drink of the cup. For
he who eats and drinks, eats and drinks judgment to himself

if he does not judge the body rightly. For this reason many among you are weak and sick, and a number sleep. But if we judged ourselves rightly, we would not be judged. But when we are judged, we are disciplined by the Lord so that we will not be condemned along with the world.
1 Corinthians 11:27-32

The Breaking of Bread Produces Unity

The early church discerned the body of the Lord in terms of Christ's huge sacrifice, and they valued it every day of their lives. They also appreciated His body made up of all the believers. Discerning the body of the Lord doesn't end with the cross. His mystical body upon the earth is also of great importance to the Lord.

Is not the cup of blessing which we bless a sharing in the blood of Christ? Is not the bread which we break a sharing in the body of Christ? Since there is one bread, we who are many are one body; for we all partake of the one bread.
1 Corinthians 10:16-17

The early church realized that breaking the bread had a supernatural power that kept the body of Christ united.

The Love of God, that bonds together all those who are His children, was put into action through this act. They not only loved one another as a body, but there was something powerful coming from Heaven that made this unity possible. It wasn't something fabricated through sermons, but something real that proceeded from the Spirit. In fact, when the Holy Spirit came upon them on the day of Pentecost, the impact of love in this outpouring was so great that it caused them to have all things in common and no one lacked anything.

As the bread is broken into pieces, it generates the opposite force; members that are separated will be attracted to form the spiritual body. The body (the bread) that is divided in the natural realm is united in the spiritual. To operate in the opposite spirit of the one we want to conquer is a spiritual principle. Through His death Jesus produced life in us. His wounded body produced health. His humility conquered pride. His true love disarmed hatred. Under this principle, the breaking of bread, symbolic of His pierced body, frees a power that supernaturally binds together those who are legitimately His church.

Upon eating the bread, we are submerged in the spiritual body of Christ throughout the world. From within it we can begin to attract each one of the parts that God has predestined to be united to us. When these precise organs converge, we will enter into our perfect function within His living organism.

Today, the body is scattered everywhere. At times its members are connected by dysfunctional joints that, far from helping us, cause us to waste away. God has a tendon, a muscle, nerves and veins precisely designed for every bone. The Lord knows which organs to put together for the stomach to digest and which parts to put around the lungs for them to breathe. The problem today is that we run behind someone's anointing, behind another's teaching, behind the traditions of others or the revival of some other place. As a result, we have an ear that is surrounded by fingers; a liver that is stuck to an eye and lungs that must go to the world's marketing system because the nose is too busy trying to force air into the kidney. Thousands of ministries are drowning, struggling to survive, trying in their flesh to generate contacts to help them. They tell one another, "I'm going to do a little public relations with these ministries because if they help me, I'll be successful." Others say, "I'm going to send all these letters to see who will help me financially." Unfortunately, everyone's mailbox is full of ministerial solicitations, asking for funds for a thousand and one causes and most solicitations remain unanswered. The reason is that the kingdom of God doesn't work this way. The Lord has predestined all the human and financial elements we require to function.

Perhaps we do not know if we are bone, tendon or muscle, but He knows. When I eat His flesh, I see His body around the world, and in this intimacy with His Spirit, I prophesy to the organs that must join me to come and supernaturally find me. I command for the divine appointments that God has preordained for me to manifest. I command the financial instruments that Jesus has already given me since before the foundation of the world to enter in contact with me. I plead the divine blood that runs in them and in me to bind us into one functional, perfect organ. I don't have to search for assistance in the most popular ministries. I have to wait on my heavenly Father and HE WILL DO IT.

The act of breaking the bread not only unites the church of one age, but it unites us to the body of Christ throughout history. We are part of a great, timeless family. The kingdom of God is eternal. Time only exists in the natural realm. There are joints in the body that are eternal, from which we can take the anointing that has remained suspended in time or reopen wells of revival that existed in other places.

Each one of us belongs to a line of anointing that stopped with the death of that wonderful someone that was supposed to pass it on to us when that someone went to be with the Lord. Perhaps you are the heir of an amazing anointing and you have never claimed it. However, eating of the bread unites it to you. You and I are simply links in a work that has continued for generations before us and that will use our lives to pass the baton to the next generation.

When Saul of Tarsus called for the stoning of Stephen, the martyr's mantel fell at his feet. Stephen forgave his executioners. When he did this, his anointing and his mission remained suspended in the air. This homicide marked Saul. When he was converted to Jesus and became part of His body, he became a debtor to those he had killed. In this act, Stephen's destiny and anointing united with Paul, who continued the work that death had interrupted.

My husband and I live in Jacksonville, the place where the first Christians landed in the United States, long before the Pilgrims arrived in New England. These believers were the French Huguenots who fled Europe during the Inquisition that was triggered off by the Reformation. When they arrived at the coast of Saint Augustine, they dedicated the land with Psalm 132, declaring that this nation would be called Zion and that it would be a country of worship to

God. Spain sent a ship with soldiers that massacred the Lord's people, leaving their mission unfinished.

In 2004, God spoke to us to recapture the destiny and work of the Huguenots that had been suspended in time. We then brought a group of the descendents of those martyrs from France. After 440 years, the Huguenots entered, singing Psalms again on the shores of the United States. As a descendent of Spaniards, I asked for their forgiveness and together we took Communion, making ourselves our brothers' debtors who died on these shores. Something very powerful came upon us from God, as we united with history through the breaking of the bread in the eternal body of Christ. We are certain that God will use us to sanctify the United States and make it once more a nation of worship.

The devil cannot erase what God has purposed. Sooner or later, God connects His body with history to establish what He has determined. What began during the Reformation is not over. What began on Azusa Street, in Wales, Pensacola, and in other places that have seen the glory of God, will again be relived by HIS BODY in this age.

There are people in the Bible or in Church history with whom we feel an extraordinary affinity. This is due to the fact that perhaps we are part of the spiritual organ that began with David or John or Paul or so many others. Our spiritual ancestors may not necessarily be members of our family by blood. For example, Benny Hinn, who clearly has over him Kathryn Kuhlman's mantle, never knew her personally nor was she his spiritual mother. However, God orchestrated a joint in heaven that birthed a powerful ministry. I have known people who when they have walked over a land for the first time, feel as if their spirit belongs to that place. It is quite possible that part of their spiritual inheritance is found in that region.

God not only wants to destroy our spiritual inheritance of evil that comes from our fathers' iniquity, but He wants us to obtain the blessed inheritance that comes from His trans-generational body.

Breaking the bread is a wonderful form of prayer that not only unites us with history, but also with the future in order to attract new believers to the body. While eating of His flesh, we should call into the body of Christ those who will form part of it.

Day by day continuing with one mind in the temple, and breaking bread from house to house, they were taking their meals together with gladness and sincerity of heart, praising God and having favor with all the people.

*And the Lord was adding to their number day by day those
who were being saved.*
Acts 2:46-47

The Breaking of Bread Builds His Tabernacle in Us

Jesus is the firstborn of all the brethren that compose
His body. He, as the Son of God, was the first living
tabernacle that housed all the fullness of God. His flesh was
the tent in which the Father and the Holy Spirit would
dwell.

God desires for that tabernacle to be built on earth
through the church. Many think that this occurs
automatically when someone says to Jesus, "Come and live
in my heart." When someone is genuinely converted the
Lord plants His seed of salvation within him, so that he
receives the authority to be called a child of God. This is the
title or family relationship that God confers on the believer
who begins to walk with Him. His dwelling will depend
upon what we do with the great treasure that He has placed
in our hands. We have the corner stone, but God wants the
finished building within us.

In that day you will know that I am in My Father, and you in Me, and I in you. He who has My commandments and keeps them is the one who loves Me; and he who loves Me will be loved by My Father, and I will love him and will disclose Myself to him. Judas (not Iscariot) said to Him, "Lord, what then has happened that You are going to disclose Yourself to us and not to the world?" Jesus answered and said to him, "If anyone loves Me, he will keep My word; and My Father will love him, and We will come to him and make Our abode with him."

John 14:20-23

Notice that the dwelling of God is not established until the believer has been proved in keeping His commandments and His Word.

Today, the condition of the church is in a grave situation. In a vast number of people, the spiritual temple of God is in ruins. God called us to be His living temple on earth, but in reality few people walk in the understanding of this high calling.

In a spiritual analogy, God showed the prophet Haggai why His people were in great lack.

Is it time for you yourselves to dwell in your paneled houses
while this house lies desolate?" Now therefore, thus says the
Lord of hosts, "Consider your ways. You have sown much,
but harvest little; you eat, but there is not enough to be
satisfied; you drink, but there is not enough to become
drunk; you put on clothing, but no one is warm enough; and
he who earns, earns wages to put into a purse with holes"...
You look for much, but behold, it comes to little: when you
bring it home, I blow it away. Why?" declares the Lord of
Hosts, "Because of My house which lies desolate, while each
of you runs to his own house.
Haggai 1:4-6; 9

This prophecy that was written referring to physical houses is also interpreted today to mean spiritual houses. Each one of us is a house, spiritual as well as anatomical or carnal. Most of our time and strength are used in building ourselves up. We are very interested in making sure that we have everything we need. Millions of prayers are just focused on "Give me, make me, help me, heal me, provide for me, fill me." In His infinite love, God gives us what we ask for in one measure or another. He fills us with His Spirit. He adorns us with spiritual gifts. He covers us with grace and favor. He cleanses us and beautifies us. Our homes are crafted by Him.

The vast majority of people in the church have taken their eyes off Jesus as the principal focus of worship and knowledge in order to serve themselves. The songs that are sung have to do with what we want from Him. Sermons focus on a better life for "us", how to reach earthly success and have victory in what we are doing. In a subtle manner, pleasing, knowing and honoring God lacks importance and our priorities replace His. Our homes are more and more ornate, and the inner temple, His dwelling place, lies forgotten and in ruins.

Learning about God from others is beautiful and necessary. However, it will never replace intimate communion with His Spirit. Knowing Him is a personal experience and it is different for every person. It is what affirms and establishes us so we cannot be shaken.

This is eternal life, that they may know You, the only true God, and Jesus Christ whom You have sent.
John 17:3

The breaking of the bread takes us to that experience of knowing Him in which our eyes are opened so we can see and our ears can hear Him.

The Lord gave the key to Haggai on how to build the temple so the Father and the Son would dwell in it:

Go up to the mountain, bring wood and rebuild the temple, that I may be pleased with it and be glorified, says the Lord.
Haggai 1:8

Wood symbolizes the human nature of Jesus, of His body. This isn't wood that can be found in the valleys, in low places, in men's "good ideas" and "good programs". It is wood from heights that are only found in the holy mountain of God. It is where the Tree of Life puts down roots to fuse with the Holy Mountain of God.

"Go up to the mountain and bring wood" is going up to the Spirit and eating of the flesh of Jesus. It is bringing everything that His body, the wood, symbolizes and making it the temple of God within us.

Each time I eat of Him, I am building His dwelling within me and He is being formed within me.

The tabernacle in the desert pointed to all Jesus would be in the flesh. The glory of God was wrapped with a cover of purity, a cover that represented His blood and a cover that symbolized the humility of His outer look. The column of fire was the visible presence of God upon the earth, settled over this tabernacle. This will also happen to those who walk in purity, humility and who are full of His blood, built into God's true temples.

The Power Contained in the Body

His Body Was Wounded to Give Us Healing and Health

When I meditate on all that Jesus conquered on the cross, I marvel that literally everything was conquered in that victory. However, it makes me sad to see that only a small few take advantage of it to live supernaturally. As I mentioned before, the number of people who are sick in the church today is dramatic. They spend thousands of dollars on medicine and hospitals when Jesus already triumphed over sickness. He is the solution, not the doctors of this world.

The big question is why the Church does not enjoy the health already purchased by her Savior?

Surely our griefs He Himself bore, and our sorrows He carried; yet we ourselves esteemed Him stricken, smitten of God, and afflicted. But He was pierced through for our transgressions. He was crushed for our iniquities; the chastening for our well-being fell upon Him, and by His scourging we are healed.
Isaiah 53:4-5

The answer is again found in understanding Communion.

In the passage of 1 Corinthians, chapter 11, we have been studying, Paul talks about health in relation to discerning Jesus' sacrifice as we participate in Communion.

For as often as you eat this bread and drink the cup, you proclaim the Lord's death until He comes. Therefore whoever eats the bread or drinks the cup of the Lord in an unworthy manner, shall be guilty of the body and the blood of the Lord. But a man must examine himself, and in so doing he is to eat of the bread and drink of the cup. For he who eats and drinks, eats and drinks judgment to himself if he does not judge the body rightly. For this reason many among you are weak and sick, and a number sleep. But if we judged ourselves rightly, we would not be judged. But when

we are judged, we are disciplined by the Lord so that we
will not be condemned along with the world.
1 Corinthians 11:26-32

Taking Communion as a ritual, without weighing in our own lives what sin, rebellion and iniquity did to Jesus puts us in a dangerous position.

Nothing causes me more pain than to think of my Lord being brutally tortured and crucified in order for us to live in health and holiness and seeing people, some running to medicine or worse, running to sin. This is like saying to Jesus, "I have better answers than yours for my health" or "I have better ways of living my life than what You designed for me."

I don't want to condemn anyone with what I'm saying, since I didn't know how to possess my health either. It was very easy for me to leave my sinful way of living because ever since I got saved I loved Jesus with all my heart. From then on, I did not want to do anything that would offend or hurt Him. But my health was a different matter. I had never seen anyone live in kingdom health. Everyone told me that God could use doctors, but something within me said that Jesus' wounds had not been in vain for me. If He had paid to conquer my sickness in such a painful way, there had to be some way to succeed in living in health.

Some theologians have calculated that the children of Israel lived around 450 years without a single person getting sick among them. This dates from the time of Moses, when they ate the bread that came down from heaven, until king Asa went to the doctor and the blessing ended. During these 450 years, radical judgments of God occurred in which God Himself caused death through sickness on specific occasions. We saw this with David and Bathsheba's child or the plague that God sent because of the census carried out by the king. However, this was a rare occurrence among the people as they lived in health.

In the thirty-ninth year of his reign Asa became diseased in his feet. His disease was severe, yet even in his disease he did not seek the Lord, but the physicians. So Asa slept with his father, having died in the forty-first year of his reign.
2 Chronicles 16:12-13

Jehovah had promised to keep His people, and He fulfilled His promise during this time. Wouldn't this promise be even more effective after Jesus carried in His body our sicknesses?

The Lord will remove from you all sickness; and He will not put on you any of the harmful diseases of Egypt which you have known, but He will lay them on all who hate you.
Deuteronomy 7:15

And He said, "If you will give earnest heed to the voice of the Lord your God, and do what is right in His sight, and give ear to His commandments, and keep all His statutes, I will put none of the diseases on you which I have put on the Egyptians; for I, the Lord, am your healer."
Exodus 15:26

I had read these passages many times. I had attended many healing crusades. I had seen God do many miracles. However, I didn't know how to enter a level in which The Cross was the only thing I needed in order to live in health. When I received the revelation I'm writing about in this book, my life changed. I began to appropriate power from Jesus' wounds for myself every time I ate of the bread.

In the spiritual world my spirit united daily with the body of Jesus, and He absorbed all my illnesses. One day we threw away all the medicine in the house and decided to live by the power of The Cross. Today, we don't even need an aspirin. We learned how to believe and to possess our inheritance. Eating His flesh, discerning and appreciating what Jesus did for us, takes us to this level of health.

The eternal life of the Almighty, living and manifesting in and through us is the true hope of glory. Our spirit, united to that of Jesus, conquers all sickness in our body. The kingdom of God subdues all matter and brings divine order to every organism.

When I feel that a sickness wants to attack my body, I take Communion and have some quiet time, allowing the Spirit of God, which is life within me, to flood my entire being. I thank Jesus for allowing Himself to be wounded and for giving His life for me. I let Him know that this was not in vain for me. No doctor has a better answer than what He did for me. If the fact of not discerning His pierced body brings judgment of sickness and death, appreciating and valuing it brings life and health.

Conquering an illness may take days, or weeks, but His power is real and His promise is true.

His Body Is the True Manna

His body is real food that sustains us and gives us strength.

Jesus then said to them, "Truly, truly, I say to you, it is not Moses who has given you the bread out of heaven, but it is My Father who gives you the true bread out of heaven. For the bread of God is that which comes down out of heaven, and gives life to the world."
John 6:32-33

Not only does the unity of our spirit with Jesus produce health, but we receive strength and vitality as well. Spiritual food provides supernatural strength in order to do great exploits for God.

People who live in the natural world don't understand where we get the vitality to carry out all the things we do in our ministry which is impossible in our own strength. We minister at conferences in around 40 countries each year. We are on television, we write books, we liberate cities, we do prophetic paintings and have recorded 10 musical CDs, and we feel 30 years younger than we are.

In previous chapters, I spoke about spiritual food and how we have been sustained in unspeakable conditions.

His Body Crucifies Our Flesh

Perhaps the greatest problem of every Christian is crucifying his flesh in order to conform to the image of the Lord.

Now those who belong to Christ Jesus have crucified the
flesh with its passions and desires.
Galatians 5:24

In Jesus resides the power to put to death every worldly desire placing it at the feet of the Father. Jesus said:

"For I have come down from heaven, not to do My own will,
but the will of Him who sent Me."
John 6:38

Jesus is the Lamb slain before the foundation of the world. When He came to earth, everything within Him spoke to Him about sacrifice. His flesh was saturated with privation and obedience to death. When we eat of His flesh, this same feeling invades our heart and our emotions. His Spirit has supernatural strength that puts His desires in our soul and makes us detest everything that does not line up with His will.

This is God's seed that lives and operates through us when we feed from the true food contained in His flesh.

No one who is born of God practices sin, because His seed abides in him; and he cannot sin, because he is born of God.
1 John 3:9

His life within us separates us from evil, it annuls the works of the devil that were constructed within us, and it conquers temptation.

It is possible to live a life of holiness. No one can offer us what our Creator gives us according to His perfect design. In Him we attain the highest purposes for our lives like fullness, joy, health, peace, prosperity and eternal life. The world with its corruption and darkness can never provide us with the things that only God can offer us.

How Does One Take Communion?

How the Early Church Took Communion

For the early church, Communion was part of the food they ate every day. It was not a religious ceremony, nor was a priest required in order to distribute it.

Day by day continuing with one mind in the temple, and breaking bread from house to house, they were taking their meals together with gladness and sincerity of heart.
Acts 2:46

We can see that it was part of their daily meals, as the Apostle Paul mentions some disorder that was present in the church of Corinth.

Therefore when you meet together, it is not to eat the Lord's Supper, for in your eating each one takes his own supper first; and one is hungry and another is drunk.
1 Corinthians 11:20-21

So then, my brethren, when you come together to eat, wait for one another. If anyone is hungry, let him eat at home, so that you will not come together for judgment.
1 Corinthians 11:33-34a

These passages show us that they ate the bread and the fruit of the vine in a simple manner, not religiously. The apostle emphasizes the need of giving this meal the spiritual sense it should have in order for it to produce life and not death.

For the early Christians it was important to talk about the Lord's death and that each of them ponders over his own life and evaluates his walk with the Lord. When one receives the bread passed on to him, he would relive in his own flesh and heart the memory of the painful sacrifice that Jesus made for the world, so that he could live a holy life for Him.

This was a meal, feeding oneself spiritually. It was not a religious ceremony, full of protocol and structure.

In the Bible there is not a single ritual relating to Communion. There is no priesthood to carry it out. It is the privilege of every believer, and it's the greatest inheritance that God gave us.

How Do We Take It?

We take Communion at home, alone as a family. Many times we get together to do it with other believers. Sometimes, we have to do it on an airplane, a restaurant or in the countryside. No matter where we take it, the Presence of the Lord manifests.

Sometimes I have to take it alone because that day no one is with me.

Some days we take a long time. We submerge ourselves in meditation about what we are doing. I like to fill myself with His blood, drinking in His wisdom. Every day is a different experience.

Most of the time, we do it in the morning, after our time of worship. Other times, we do it at night before going to bed. That way I can enjoy His presence all night long. But there are other times that we don't take much time, just enough to be in deep contact with our Savior and go on.

It is not a ritual. It is life. What is life is not planned; one lives and enjoys the glorious moments it offers.

In churches or retreats where we have taught this topic, we put the elements at the entrance so that each person can pick it up, and then we take Communion together during worship or at the end of the service.

In this book I tell a small part of the thousands of experiences and revelations that the Lord has given me through Communion. Telling all of them would take many volumes.

My prayer is that you can receive from the Lord what He has left us in this marvelous Supper, which is true food and true drink. Thousands of lives have been transformed upon entering in to possess their true celestial inheritance.

He who eats My flesh and drinks My blood abides in Me,
and I in him. As the living Father sent Me, and I live because
of the Father, so he who eats Me, he also will live
because of Me.
John 6:56-57

Let's fill the earth with a generation full of Jesus' life!

Bibliography

Bridge, Donald and Phypers, David,
Communion: The Meal that Unites,

Bromiley, G.W., ed., Zwingli and Bullinger

Calvin, John, Institutes of the Chrstian Religion, ed. by J.T. McNeill

Edwards, Gene, The Day I Was Crucified

Leadbeater, C. W., La Vida Oculta de la Masoneria

McDonnell, K., John Calvin, The Church, and the Eucharist

Pelikan, J. and Lehmann, H.T., eds., Luther's Works

Schaff, P., ed., "The Canons and Decrees of the Council of Trent," in Creeds of Christendom, II

Tracts relating to Reformation